D1626967

A NEW
HUMANITY

A NEW HUMANITY

Embracing
Our Responsibility
for the Earth

ILCHI LEE

BEST
LIFE
MEDIA

BEST
LIFE
MEDIA

459 N. Gilbert Rd, A-275
Gilbert, AZ 85234
www.BestLifeMedia.com
480-926-2480

Copyright © 2023 by Ilchi Lee

All rights reserved. No part of this book may be reproduced or transmitted in any form or by any means, electronic or mechanical, including photocopying, recording, or by any information storage or retrieval system, without permission in writing from the publisher.

Please understand that this book is not intended to treat, cure, or prevent any disease or illness. The information in this book is intended for educational purposes only, not as medical advice. Always check with your health professional before changing your diet, eating, or health program. The author and publisher disclaim any liability arising directly or indirectly from the use and application of any of the book's contents.

First paperback edition: November 2023
Library of Congress Control Number: 2023945545
ISBN-13: 978-1-947502-27-7

Cover and interior design by Kiryl Lysenka

To my fellow Earth Citizens who believe
in the goodness of humanity

CONTENTS

INTRODUCTION

Anticipating the Birth of a New Humanity

During this spring and summer, I traveled to four continents. My path took me from New Zealand to South Korea and Japan, onward to Spain and France in Europe, and finally to my home in the United States. I aimed to connect with Brain Education practitioners and my readers, facilitating workshops and retreats along the way.

During my journey, one clear theme kept coming up, no matter where or who I was talking to—the urgent climate crisis. Everywhere I went, in every conversation, people were concerned about our planet's *crazy* weather and the steady rise in temperatures.

Earlier this year, New Zealand was hit hard by heavy rains. At one point, the rain in a single day was as much as 70 percent of what usually falls over three months in past years. It felt like the rain pierced the sky, leading to flooding and the partial closure of Auckland International Airport.

When I reached South Korea, an intense heat wave was sweeping the area. Officials issued heat wave alerts for different parts of the country, and we often saw warnings for both heat waves and heavy rain multiple times a day. Before long, heavy rainfall caused an underground tunnel to flood, leading to a tragic loss of lives. At the same time, Japan was facing a similar situation. Unprecedented rain hit some areas, while others faced intense heat waves. In just one week, Tokyo alone saw over 50 cases of heatstroke.

Barely had I arrived in Spain when I was jolted by the news of a ferocious fire devouring the Greek island of Rhodes. A parallel situation was unfolding at my home in Arizona, USA. The temperature stayed over 110 degrees for over a month; even the resilient saguaro cacti couldn't withstand the heat. There were also huge forest fires in nearby California and Nevada, burning mountains larger than half of Seoul. As I finalize this manuscript, an unusual hurricane has caused flooding on the west coast of North America, and wildfires in Hawaii have caused tragic loss of human life and historical buildings.

Throughout the trip, I deeply felt the harsh reality our Earth is dealing with right now. It's not limited to one country or city. Severe events that used to be rare, happening maybe every 50 or 100 years, have become a global norm. We see these disasters in the news so often that they don't surprise us anymore.

The UN Secretary-General has declared: "The era of global warming has ended; the era of global boiling has arrived." In July 2023, 81 percent of the world's population experienced heat waves, as reported by the climate research group Climate Central. Destructive heat waves and floods have devastated crops and economies, with productivity taking a hit. The financial impact of climate change is surpassing experts' predictions, leaving them astonished by its gravity.

No single person can be blamed for this situation. It's not just the leaders making policies; everyone who lives and breathes on this planet plays a role. Whether knowingly or not, our actions, big and small, have shaped the world we see today.

It's not just the climate crisis. Other serious issues like wealth inequality, global conflicts, escalating violence, and social unrest result from people's collective choices and actions in our time. We must face this truth honestly and acknowledge our responsibility to our planet and all life. Mere thoughts won't be enough; our acknowledgment and responsibility must resonate deeply within us, awakening our core and driving us to make genuine changes in our daily lives.

No one knows how much time we have, but one thing is clear. The pace of the changes we are worried about, including climate change, is accelerating faster than ever. As the challenges for our planet are growing, the time to tackle them is dwindling. This means we need to step up and make fundamental and radical changes.

Imagine a big shift, like the birth of a new species in evolution's story. Biological changes take ages, but shifts in thoughts and consciousness can happen in an instant. The key is to act with urgency and determination. If we truly feel the need for change and decide to act, our thoughts and consciousness can switch quickly.

If many people make these changes together, it won't just be individual change. It can lead to the creation of an entirely new species. It's like the birth of a new humanity with different consciousness and behaviors. The current problems on Earth demand this level of change. We need a society that understands the interconnectedness of all living beings and prioritizes coexistence over self-interest. I want to call it *Homo coexistence*.

New Humanity Pledge

In line with these aspirations, I introduced the New Humanity Pledge after publishing my book *The Art of Coexistence*. The pledge aims to mobilize individuals worldwide to take responsibility for creating coexistence on Earth. It has been embraced in 16 countries, serving as a call to action for necessary change.

The essence of the New Humanity Pledge can be expressed in one simple sentence: "I pledge to become part of a new humanity and to make creating coexistence on Earth my personal responsibility and priority."

Becoming part of the new humanity means adopting a new set of values and ways of life. It may require stepping out of our comfort zones, choosing discomfort over convenience, and making difficult decisions that benefit the greater good over personal gain. It means confirming within ourselves that we are ready and willing to make these changes.

Making coexistence with Earth our responsibility means thinking about it every day and integrating it into our daily lives. If we see it as our responsibility, we can't use the excuse, "Others aren't doing it." And if we prioritize it, we can't delay action by saying, "Let me finish my other important things first."

Taking responsibility for coexistence with Earth means treating it as seriously as paying our bills or caring for dependent children. It means making the health and well-being of the Earth a core value that guides everything we consider important.

Like all other life-forms, we have received the gift of life from nature. In the presence of nature, all humanity is one undivided family, and all forms of life are interconnected. Everything is intertwined as a whole, with no isolation. We all must grasp this undeniable truth to our core and transform into a new humanity that cares for and protects all life.

This book serves as both an explanation and practical guide for the New Humanity Pledge. If you're hearing about it for the first time, I hope it inspires you to join us and ignites that inner passion to contribute to a better world. And if you're already part of the pledge, this book will help you integrate it into your life and create true *Homo coexistence*.

I Give Birth to Myself

The power to create a peaceful, just, and sustainable world of coexistence lies within every one of us. Our awareness, choices, and actions can bring about the change we desire. I refer to this awakening as "I give birth to myself."

Our physical bodies are born once, a gift from our parents. There's not much we can do to start our physical lives over again. However, we can recreate our consciousness anytime we choose through a process of self-birth. This journey starts with telling yourself, "I am a being with the power to choose, change, and grow." We are independent beings who can fully realize our unique potential. Embracing this belief, we unearth our intrinsic value and shape our destiny. Through this unshakable faith, we lead a life of genuine self-creation—nurturing our passions, holding onto hope, and giving rise to a new self each day.

The birth of a new humanity starts with each of us rediscovering our personal worth and recognizing the value of every human being. Our dreams and ambitions must breathe life into these values. As humans, we have the amazing ability to pursue the greater good beyond our own interests; it's our greatest strength. Do we each have the determination to believe in ourselves, shape our own futures, and make positive contributions to a better world? If we do, then as a united humanity, we can build unshakable mutual trust, taking charge of our collective destiny.

Our collective choices have never before held such immense power to reshape the Earth's course and future. Past generations believed the planet's resources were limitless and that the Earth is eternal. But for us, the present generation, the Earth's fate hinges on our actions. In this era, including both you and me, we stand as the first to witness how our choices can completely transform the Earth and humanity during our lifetime. You and I have the power to save or imperil our planet.

You hold the power to change the world. Never let go of that knowledge. If you believe in your power to change your life, you can change the world as well. Let us anchor our faith in a better future for humanity. Let us never lose hope in creating a more peaceful, mindful, and sustainable world. As long as we keep nurturing our dreams and hopes for a better life and world, they will uplift and push us forward.

Dreams and hopes can turn aimless wanderings into thrilling adventures, ignite passion instead of lethargy, and unite scattered, lonely hearts as one. Hope isn't reserved solely for times of ease; it's most crucial during the toughest challenges. In broad daylight, even hundreds of candles might not stand out. But in the darkest night, even a single candle offers guidance. Right now, we need not just one or two but thousands, tens of thousands, and millions of candles. I genuinely believe you are one of those guiding lights.

The future that the New Humanity Pledge envisions doesn't simply unfold on its own. It's not a distant scenario we just watch or worry about. Instead, it's a future we actively create with our intentions, choices, and actions. Becoming a new humanity means consciously opting to live as our current selves, free from the constraints of our past. It's about each of us, as individuals, taking action *today*, facing our planet's and humanity's present reality, and bringing about change. The miracle of you and I saving the Earth doesn't rely on grand events. Our hope is grounded in the small, everyday changes we commit to. Together, we can give birth to *Homo coexistence* by renewing ourselves every day and inspiring each other with our awakened consciousness and meaningful actions.

Through this book, I hope that you become a part of this new humanity, joining in what could be the most significant human endeavor ever—crafting a peaceful and sustainable world through our efforts.

Ilchi Lee

CHAPTER 1

Why a New Humanity?

I often pose these questions to people: "What are the biggest challenges in your life?" and "What causes you the most stress?" The answers I receive tend to follow a familiar pattern. People typically mention work, finances, family, health, and planning for retirement. However, a new element is seeping into their responses: uncertainty. A sense of unpredictability and lack of control over life's unfolding changes is becoming increasingly common.

Throughout history, both personally and culturally, people have faced new challenges and changes. Previous generations also believed the world was in danger. But today's challenges are distinctly different from those of the past. In the old days, many threats developed over time and were confined to specific regions. But now, everything moves at incredible speed, spreads globally, and has far-reaching consequences. The impact of these challenges is deeply and directly felt in our daily lives. The risks we face now are on a whole new level.

Take climate change, for instance. It transcends borders and affects every corner of the globe, leading to extreme weather events, melting ice caps, and disruptive effects on agriculture and economies. While climate change is a global concern, its impacts are keenly felt in our day-to-day experiences.

In the spring of 2023, high temperatures and drought unleashed the worst wildfires ever seen in Canada. For months, a multitude of uncontrollable wildfires blazed simultaneously across the country. By June, the smoke had drifted to the eastern United States, painting the sky an eerie orange and even crossing the Atlantic to Europe. As I write this book in early August, the wildfires have consumed an area equivalent to the state of Georgia and remain uncontained.

A few days ago, the news broadcasted a gut-wrenching scene: Maui, Hawaii, a place I hold dear, became engulfed in flames. Victims of the rapidly spreading inferno, who lost homes and loved ones, sat in stunned silence at evacuation shelters. Their struggle brought to mind the recent tragedy of floods and landslides South Korea faced this summer. Climate change-driven disasters are tearing lives apart across the globe, a harsh reality underscored by these ongoing events.

In addition to climate instability, our social and financial structures seem to have weakened. Earlier this year, there was a bank run at a bank in Silicon Valley, USA. Worried depositors withdrew their money from the bank all at once. The situation was so severe that the US Federal Reserve and Treasury had to step in, guaranteeing full payment to prevent further panic. The fear spread to an eastern US bank and eventually reached the second-largest bank in Switzerland. It was the first time since the Great Depression in the 1930s that we saw the possibility of a chain bank run becoming a reality. Luckily, swift intervention from the Swiss, EU, and US governments and international financial institutions prevented the situation from escalating further. If the response had been delayed even slightly, it could have led to a collapse of the global financial system.

These events, like the COVID-19 pandemic, have shown us how connected and vulnerable our social systems can be when faced with unexpected changes. Amidst all these challenges, one significant source of uncertainty is the rapid rise of new artificial intelligence (AI) technologies.

Do you remember the surprising arrival of ChatGPT? This generative AI, introduced in November

2022, has broken all previous records for application user growth. Within just a week, it had over a million users, and within two months, it reached a staggering 100 million users. ChatGPT can engage in conversations, write, draw, compose music, make videos, and even code. Its applications are expanding rapidly, including professional medical diagnoses, business analysis, and legal advice. As predicted, it is rapidly replacing human jobs, especially in tech, marketing, and social media content creation. While many were initially fascinated by its capabilities, some now harbor feelings of concern and fear about its impact.

This AI technology operates in fascinating ways, akin to the complex neural network of the human brain, and it accomplishes remarkable feats. However, despite its achievements, we still don't fully understand how it all works. As the AI network expands, it develops new skills such as suddenly being able to speak a language it hasn't been explicitly taught. It's puzzling how these abilities emerge. This uncertainty has led to concerns about the potential for unforeseen and uncontrollable AI capabilities. In fact, there was a call for AI regulation in May, with support from experts in the field, including the CEO of OpenAI, the company behind ChatGPT.

There have already been extensive discussions on the challenges and risks that humanity faces, and plenty of information is available. The more important thing is to understand the roles and responsibilities we can take on to tackle them. Everyone in this era experiences the direct impact of these risks and is responsible for addressing them. Without awareness and action from each of us, these problems cannot be solved.

Many people think they don't have much to contribute regarding these issues. They often believe the solutions must come from fancy new technologies, global political agreements, or new laws and institutions, such as using innovative technologies to reduce CO_2 levels, signing agreements to limit carbon emissions, or regulating the development and use of AI technology.

But is that really how it works? Think about the Paris Agreement, for example. It was supposed to be a game-changer in limiting carbon emissions, but it seems to have lost momentum and turned into a polished document gathering dust. And when it comes to AI technology, we hear a lot of talk about the need for regulations, but behind the scenes, it's more about each player trying to win the competition to seize opportunities. Even if we wanted to regulate, there's a lack of trust among the leading companies and countries in this field. They're too busy competing for technological dominance to work together on setting meaningful standards.

While new environmental technologies and technological standards can undoubtedly help, they aren't the ultimate solutions to these problems. Climate change and the uncertainties surrounding emerging technologies aren't the root causes; they're the consequences of deeper issues. We need to look closer, beyond the atmosphere, big data, and computer algorithms, to find the underlying causes.

What Do We Really Want?

At its core, this issue boils down to what we are interested in and desire in life. Regardless of our outward interests, one common sense fact is that people invest their time, attention, and resources into what truly matters to them.

It's like those personalized online ads that seem to know our preferences exactly. The data we leave behind paints the most objective and candid picture of what we like, value, and desire. This information reflects my preferences, from the posts, photos, and products I engage with, to the articles and ads I click on. When content is customized based on this data, it effectively captures my attention and engages me.

If we were to think of our desires as arrows, each pointing in a different direction with varying strengths, where do you think all our desires will lead us? Are we moving toward a peaceful and sustainable future, or are we being pulled in the opposite direction?

Take the recent advancements in AI technologies, for example. We're caught up in a whirlwind of changes, swept along without a clear idea of where it's all heading. Even the leaders in the field are racing to keep up without a full grasp of the long-term consequences. We might believe we're simply trying to understand and adapt to these changes or that systems, markets, trends, or some mysterious force beyond our control drive them. Those thoughts might momentarily ease our concerns or alleviate our guilt.

However, everyone living today participates in these problems through active acceptance or resistance, passive adaptation, or implicit consent. No one is exempt from the consequences of these changes. And deep down, we know that every situation unfolding on Earth is ultimately the result of our collective choices and actions based on our interests and desires.

What are the primary motivators behind our decisions to adopt new technologies, systems, or rules? Why do people rush to buy the latest gadgets or tools? Well, convenience plays a big part. Business owners adopt new technologies to streamline operations and boost profits. Politicians passionately campaign and voice their beliefs to gain power.

Convenience, profits, and power—they drive our decisions when it comes to embracing new technologies or systems. Suppose something promises to make our lives easier, bring us greater financial gains, or increase our societal influence. In that case, we're likely to go for it, as long as it's not illegal, immoral, or disreputable—even if it means bending the rules a bit.

Imagine approaching someone on a scorching summer day, watching them sip their iced coffee from a disposable cup with a plastic straw, and telling them they're contributing to environmental destruction. Chances are, they won't readily accept that notion. They probably just wanted a convenient and refreshing drink without any harmful intentions toward the planet. Similarly, who can blame entrepreneurs for seeking profits in a market-driven economy? Under a democratic system with representative political institutions and elections, who can question a politician's pursuit of power to fulfill their vision or ambition?

We each need to ask ourselves a simple, straightforward question: "If it would benefit the Earth, would I be willing to sacrifice some convenience, profit, or power?" It's a question that requires an honest answer. Our planet's and humanity's future doesn't depend solely on new technologies or systems. It rests on our individual responses to this question.

Ultimately, our answers are intertwined with the values we prioritize in life. Depending on the values we hold dear, making sacrifices for the Earth can bring deep satisfaction or pose challenging and painful loss. If our focus revolves solely around convenience, profits, and power, it might be challenging to say "yes" to this question. However, our choices will take a different shape if we seek personal growth and collective well-being beyond material gains. In that sense, our answers to this question indicate our individual awareness and sincerity and the overall maturity of human civilization.

The Limits of Intelligence

Intelligence has always been seen as the defining characteristic that sets us humans apart from other species. That's why we call ourselves *Homo sapiens*, the "wise man." Intelligence is present in every aspect of our lives, from basic survival skills like hunting to creative endeavors like art. And among its many values, problem-solving abilities are crucial.

Thanks to our intelligence, we've solved countless problems throughout history. It has brought us to where we are today, with all our scientific advancements and technological marvels. We've come a long way and still benefit from human genius today.

However, it has had unintended consequences. Our intelligence has led to all the challenges our current human society faces, and it has created the problems we have caused for the Earth's environment and other forms of life. Suppose we had evolved more like other primates. We probably wouldn't have caused so many problems with our human activities. If the superior abilities of humans compared to other species lead to self-destruction, they could be considered foolish rather than intelligent. Can it indeed be considered intelligence if the evolutionary journey of *Homo sapiens* leads to self-destruction? These are questions that remain unanswered, awaiting the ultimate judgment.

One of the distinguishing characteristics and limitations of our intelligence is its divisive and self-centered nature. In essence, the limits of our intelligence are the limits of our ego. We tend to focus our intelligence on actions that benefit us directly. Even when scientists measure the intelligence of other animals, they often use this same yardstick. But sometimes, in our pursuit of self-interest, we make choices that harm others, disregarding their suffering and even destroying the environment that sustains all lives. We do this very frequently and effectively. These choices and actions manifest as hostility, aggression, social injustice, discrimination, environmental pollution, and the destruction of ecosystems.

This limitation is more a result of our current perception and values than an inherent flaw of intelligence itself. Throughout history, we've been mired in the mindset of seeing ourselves as separate individuals, constantly competing and struggling. Now and then, spiritual teachings have emerged like oases in the desert, reminding us of love and compassion. But even those messages often create more conflicts and disagreements than harmony as people mold them to fit their own purposes.

We've seen so many amazing things that should have shifted our perception, like the beautiful, fragile image of Earth from space or the mind-blowing discoveries of modern physics showing us how everything is connected and influencing each other. But we can't seem to break free from this self-centered way of thinking. Our intelligence is trapped within this framework, which is all about the ego. And as long as we keep operating within this framework, it's hard to expect different outcomes. If we truly want a change, we must shift our perception and break free from this self-centered mindset.

But here's the tricky part. The belief that we are separate individuals and that life is a constant battle is not an illusion or misinterpretation. It's the reality we face every day. Throughout our long evolutionary history, humans have had to compete with different species or tribes and adapt to unpredictable environmental changes. It's how we survived and evolved. This perception of being separate individuals and the self-centered thinking that comes with it isn't just some personal trait or limitation; it's deeply ingrained in our history.

And you can see how our daily realities reinforce this perception. We experience it in our packed subway trains where we squeeze and push to make room for ourselves, in the traffic jams where we fight for any bit of space, in the cutthroat competition starting from elementary school onward, and in the tough job market for fresh graduates. With all that going on, is it even possible to see beyond this individualistic framework of confrontation and competition? That's the limit of our current intelligence, a challenge we're facing head-on.

Asking the Right Questions

The limitations of knowledge are becoming apparent as our self-centered and purely pragmatic intellect reaches its boundaries. It's interesting how the role of knowledge, which is intelligence's content, is changing significantly. With the rise of AI, knowledge has become easily accessible to everyone. We used to think that "knowledge is power," but now it's not as accurate as it once seemed. We live in an era where all the knowledge in the world is right at our fingertips, like the water and air that we consume daily. AI already affects many knowledge-based jobs, and more machines will take over human activities in the coming years.

In this changing landscape, what truly matters is asking the right questions that lead us to the knowledge we seek. The ability to ask the right questions is more important than simply storing answers in the brain. When we ask the right questions, we're more likely to discover the right answers. If we ask dumb questions, we'll end up with trash answers. AI can provide solutions, but the act of questioning is something uniquely human.

So, what does it take to ask the right questions?

First of all, we need to acknowledge and embrace our ignorance. To ask the right questions, we need to know what we don't know. It starts by recognizing and admitting our ignorance. As the wise philosopher Socrates emphasized with his famous saying, "Know thyself," acknowledging our own ignorance marks the initial step toward learning and wisdom. However, if we think we already know everything or should know everything, we close off the space for curiosity and inquiry.

If the universe were a sandy beach, the Earth would be smaller than a single grain of sand. In fact, there's so much about our planet that we don't know compared to what we do know. We've pretty much explored every corner of the land on Earth, including those frosty polar regions. But we still have much to discover regarding the vast oceans covering 71 percent of our planet's surface. The number of people who have been to the Mariana Trench, the deepest part of Earth's crust, is fewer than those who have been to the Moon.

We can only explain less than 5 percent of all the matter and energy in the universe. The other 95 percent is some mysterious substance called dark matter and dark energy. Even with all our knowledge, there's still so much we don't know, and that's okay. It's essential to realize and accept our own ignorance. Doing so doesn't mean we're incompetent or lacking; rather, it is a sign of wisdom and maturity.

The second requirement after asking the right questions is to stay open to new answers and to cultivate curiosity about untapped possibilities. Even when we ask the right questions and find brilliant answers, they won't be much help if we're stuck in our ways and resistant to new ideas and changes. Our assumptions and biases get in the way. Some of these biases are so deeply rooted in us that we don't notice them until they're challenged. Our familiar beliefs and biases make it hard to embrace new answers because we see them as absolute facts woven into who we are.

One of the most famous examples in history is the Copernican Revolution. It changed how we saw the universe, shifting from the idea that the Earth is the center to understanding that our planets orbit the Sun. Copernicus wrote a book about this heliocentric model in 1543, but it took a really long time for it to be accepted. The Church's ban on the book endured until 1757, and it wasn't until 1822 that supporting works could be published. Despite all the evidence, it took centuries of debates and persecution for people to embrace the idea that the Earth isn't at the center of everything.

A more recent example is how we've come to understand and address climate change as a pressing global issue. Scientists have been gathering evidence, and meteorologists have been sounding the alarm for decades. However, it took a while for most of society to recognize and accept the reality of climate change truly. Our personal biases, preconceived notions, and economic and political interests created obstacles along the way.

We're always asking "why?" because we're naturally curious and have an innate desire to know. Even Albert Einstein, widely recognized as an intelligence icon, once said, "I don't have any special talents. I'm just passionately curious." But curiosity alone isn't always enough to push us through the challenges, obstacles, and discomfort that come with seeking answers.

To keep asking questions and searching for solutions, we need to have hopes and dreams. These qualities become even more critical regarding our own real-life situations. We ask questions about our reality, not just to gain more knowledge. It's because we are unsatisfied with how things are and want to explore better possibilities.

So, the third prerequisite for asking the right questions is to hold on to hope for better possibilities. Questions don't come from a heart that's given up. The deepest inquiries arise from hearts brimming with dreams and hopes; we ask the most profound questions when we have dreams and hopes. This is true for humanity's current situation on Earth too. We question because we believe we can do better than the expected outcomes and create a brighter future.

The right questions can only arise when we have enough humility to admit our ignorance, when we have open minds and curiosity about new possibilities, and when we have a passionate drive to create a better tomorrow. These qualities may seem different from, or even contrary to, what we typically consider part of intelligence—like understanding, analyzing, and retaining information. However, these qualities help us rise above the limitations of intellect and guide us toward wisdom. They help us find fresh new answers to the challenges we face.

The World Needs Wisdom

Wisdom takes us beyond the limits of self-centered intellect. It's all about seeing the interconnectedness between things that may seem separate initially, the connection between unrelated objects, or the links between distant events. We often call this ability to see deep associations insight, the gift of wisdom.

Wisdom is inherent to the human mind and accessible to everyone. It's not about how smart or capable we are. Intelligence driven solely by self-interest won't solve the world's problems; in fact, it can worsen the situation. To tap into wisdom, we must ask ourselves some important questions: "How can I help others, not just myself?" and "How can I contribute to the greater good?" These questions open new possibilities and activate different parts of our minds, leading to wisdom and fresh insights.

Wisdom emerges through the interplay of our intellectual capacities for thinking and judgment and noble qualities of the human heart, like self-reflection, conscience, and empathy. The capacity for wisdom exists within us all, but unfortunately, many haven't had the chance to fully manifest it due to the dominance of their self-centered intellect. But the world needs wisdom now more than ever.

Recognizing the limitations of self-centered intellect and seeking answers from a broader perspective that considers the world's well-being isn't about changing systems or institutions. It's a deeply personal transformation that happens within each of us. The change we need is both global and profoundly personal. It requires a substantial shift within every individual, and it must happen on a global scale.

A Special Time We Are Living In

In March 2023, the Intergovernmental Panel on Climate Change (IPCC) released its 6th report on climate change. This report is the culmination of all the previous reports and represents a comprehensive understanding of the topic. It officially recognizes that human activities are responsible for the current climate change, although some still disagree.

The new report doesn't provide us with a lot of fresh information. It mainly brings together and solidifies what we already understand about climate change. For example, even if we significantly reduce our reliance on fossil fuels, the temperatures in the atmosphere and oceans will keep rising. As a result, climate patterns will undergo accelerated changes. However, the extent of the temperature increase can still be influenced by the actions we take.

According to the report, climate change scenarios between 2030 and 2050 can be divided into three main possibilities: a temperature rise of about 1.5 degrees Celsius, 2 degrees Celsius, or possibly even higher. To reach the goal of keeping the temperature increase within the desired limit of 1.5 degrees and avoid the worst impacts of climate change, we must cut our CO_2 emission in half by 2030 and achieve net zero, which means zero increase of CO_2 in the atmosphere, by 2050. It's a tough challenge, but climate experts believe it's not impossible.

The report mentions a few more factors that play a role in rising temperatures. One of them is the release of methane from thawing permafrost. As the frozen ground thaws, it releases a significant amount of methane, a potent greenhouse gas. Another factor is the reduction of reflectivity in polar regions. With the ice caps melting, less sunlight gets reflected back into space, causing further warming. We also have carbon emissions from wildfires, which release carbon dioxide when forests burn during extreme heat and drought.

Additionally, there are limitations to how much carbon the oceans and land can absorb, and as they reach their limits, more greenhouse gases stay in the atmosphere. Lastly, as the marine ecosystem suffers from seawater acidification, it severely hampers the ocean's ability to absorb carbon dioxide through phytoplankton. This sets off a harmful cycle, leading to further increases in atmospheric carbon dioxide.

So, it's not just about fossil fuels. These additional factors are also part of the puzzle regarding rising temperatures and climate change. We need to address all of them if we want to make a real difference.

These changes we're talking about aren't just some far-off predictions; they're happening on a large scale right now. Some of these changes can't be undone even if we try to slow them down. Thus, the report focuses on *mitigation*, which means taking action to lessen the impact rather than just preventing or restoring things.

Experts have some suggestions for how we can mitigate these effects. They suggest things like capturing carbon, using cleaner sources of energy, planting more trees, and putting a tax on carbon emissions. But even if we do all of that, we won't be able to fully stop or reverse these changes. Our actions can only help reduce their impact.

The report also emphasizes the need for *adaptation* as another significant action. We must accept that change will happen and prepare to roll with it. This includes growing crops that can withstand harsh climates, creating new habitats and spaces, and setting up emergency systems to deal with floods and other climate-related disasters. The report makes it clear that mitigating the impact and adapting to climate change require everyone, every country, and every individual to get involved immediately.

The good news is that concerning technology, we've got what it takes to tackle both mitigation and adaptation. We already have the knowledge and tools to implement all the recommended measures. So, the real challenge isn't about technology. It's about getting everyone on board, all around the world, to take immediate and proactive actions for change. If we fail to rise to this challenge, it won't be because we misunderstand the problem, don't know the solutions, or lack the necessary resources. It will simply be because we didn't unite and make the right choices together. The consequences of such an outcome would be regrettable and disheartening.

The clock is ticking, and while we can't predict precisely how much time remains, one thing is certain: the pace of the changes we worry about, particularly with climate change, is intensifying every day. The enormity of the problem leaves us with less and less time to find solutions. To meet this challenge, we must take bold and immediate actions. It demands a global transformative shift, along with a personal shift that touches the consciousness and behavior of each individual. As we confront this urgent reality, the need for radical and rapid changes has never been more crucial.

We're living in a time like no other in human history. Our collective choices can shape our planet's future and humanity's destiny. We're the first generation to witness and possibly the last to experience the full impact of the changes happening in our lifetime. If we make the right choices and transform our consciousness, we can spare future generations from carrying the weight of these concerns. However, if we fail to overcome this crisis and our civilization reaches a point of no return, even the need for future generations to worry about these issues would become meaningless. This makes our lifetime exceptional and makes each of us living in this era incredibly special.

The Changes We Need

All mammals, including humans, have evolved from a common ancestor over a period of 100 million years. Surprisingly, the genetic changes during all those years make up less than 10 percent of our genetic makeup. We have more than 90 percent of our genes in common with other mammals like dogs, mice, cows, and elephants. The genetic differences between individuals within the same race are much more significant than those between different races. No matter who you encounter while walking down the street, even if they belong to another race or culture, your genetic difference is less than 0.01 percent.

Even if we look back in time, the story remains the same. Modern humans have been around for approximately 300,000 years, and there haven't been any major biological changes during this time. This genetic stability is because our ability to use tools and technology has decreased the necessity for physical adaptations to ensure our survival.

The changes that have happened during this time are not physical ones. The most fundamental changes have occurred in our consciousness, thoughts, and behaviors. In more recent history, we've witnessed significant transformations that have reshaped our worldview. The scientific revolution questioned Earth's place in the universe, religious reforms changed beliefs and made religion personal, and civil revolutions gave citizens the power to shape society.

These moments have completely reshaped how we see gods, the universe, Earth, ourselves, and our relationships with others. These changes started in our consciousness, and they have had a much more significant impact on our lives and the world around us than the slow and gradual adaptations that happened over thousands or millions of years.

It's time for another change in our consciousness, thinking, and behavior. This change must go beyond superficial adjustments and reach deep into our hearts. It calls for us to ask profound questions about our identity, values, purpose, and the world we envision. We need a swift and far-reaching transformation that spans the globe comparable to the sudden genetic mutations that shape the course of evolution.

Fortunately, technological advancements and an inclusive mindset toward diversity create favorable circumstances for such changes. Unlike in the past, where a single trend prevailed, we now see various modes of thinking and living emerge and fade simultaneously. And with the rise of digital technology, distance and time are no longer barriers. Similar trends and styles can pop up in entirely different parts of the world.

Many things can bring people together. It could be a shared love for fashion or art, various political beliefs, and the technology we rely on, like communication devices and platforms. We even have generational labels like Generation X or Generation Z that reflect how technology shapes our mindset and lifestyle as we grow up. These factors create social networks and communities where people think and act in unique ways, especially united by a common interest or goal. Given the current crisis we're facing, which threatens the values we cherish on Earth, we are strongly motivated to come together and make collective change.

If all these changes happen together with the choices we consciously make, it's like witnessing the birth of a new tribe or even a whole new kind of people. These individuals would have a different way of thinking, consciousness, and behaviors compared to the past. The challenges we currently face on Earth require a transformation of such magnitude. We need the emergence of a new kind of humanity that we can call Homo coexistence. This new humanity would understand and value the interconnectedness between all living beings, prioritize coexistence over self-interest, and make decisions and take action accordingly.

Unlike biological changes that take a long time, shifts in consciousness and thinking can happen in a blink of an eye. It's incredible how a moment of awareness or decision can completely transform someone's life or even lead to miraculous healing. The key is to feel a sense of urgency and be determined to bring about change. When we truly grasp the need for change and make a conscious choice, our thinking and consciousness can shift quickly. By embracing new perspectives and adopting new behaviors, we have the power to transform our lives. And when many individuals join in this transformation, we can change the course of our entire civilization.

CHAPTER 2

We Need a Better Story

Where do we start to bring about a new humanity with fresh consciousness, thoughts, and behaviors? How can we initiate personal change that resonates globally on our planet? I believe the first step is creating a new story for ourselves. Most of us are already aware that the planet is in crisis and urgent change is necessary. However, the real challenge is translating this awareness into actionable thoughts and behaviors.

We need to weave a story together that deeply resonates with our hearts and inspire deliberate action. If we unite our efforts, we can create a narrative that motivates us to choose a sustainable lifestyle and to prioritize the well-being of all life instead of short-term convenience, profit, and power. This story must become a constant presence in our minds. The New Humanity Pledge and this book both strive to build and share such a narrative.

Stories are the primary means by which we give meaning to our lives. One special trait that sets us apart from other animals is our quest for meaning. Meaning holds significance not just for individual lives, but also for communities, guiding life's purpose and direction. We're naturally inclined to derive meaning from our experiences by shaping them into stories and sharing them with others. No one exists without a story. Whether aware of it or not, humans are innate storytellers.

If you've ever raised kids or spent time with little ones, you know how incredible they are at spinning tales and how much they enjoy it. When kids start telling stories, they don't always separate their made-up stories from what's real. They genuinely believe their stories are true, and they can laugh and cry based on the stories they create. As we grow older, our stories become more intricate, and we learn to distinguish between reality and fiction. But deep down, we're still driven by the search for meaning, and the stories we tell continue to shape us.

Because we're always making and sharing stories, they can sometimes seem like flights of fancy or simple entertainment. However, stories are more than just figments of imagination or fiction. They mirror our real experiences and values, serving as powerful tools to help us understand our own purpose and place in the world. They let us express emotions, share ideas, and connect with others socially. It's fascinating how storytelling is rooted in our very nature and has a massive impact on us. We use it in many ways, including in politics, marketing, education, and even how organizations are run and consulted.

An experience isn't just a simple record of what happened. How we perceive, understand, and give meaning to those events influences it. It's also shaped by how we react to them. What truly shapes my identity isn't just the events that have unfolded in my life but how I interpret and weave them into the story in my memory. In that sense, I am my story, especially the story I choose to tell. That story can make me resent and doubt my own life, or it can infuse it with meaning, open up new possibilities, and spark grand visions.

The Story That Humanity Has Continued

Throughout history, humans have been shaped by all sorts of stories. Some of these stories go beyond our personal experiences and reflect what we desire, fear, and believe about the meaning of our existence as a tribe or as a species. Despite our different backgrounds and cultures, these stories have similar patterns. They're like blueprints that show up in various forms across different cultures. Psychologists and anthropologists call them archetypes, and they greatly impact how we see the world and our place in it. From ancient myths to the stories we find in books and movies today, they inspire us, give us new perspectives, and shape how we think and act.

As for the stories that define us today, humanity is surrounded by diverse narratives. Many stories focus on competition, conflict, domination, and power struggles. Economic and political systems, media, and popular culture build and reinforce these narratives. Sadly, most stories of simple happiness and personal contentment fade away with individual lives and are hardly passed down as meaningful tales.

As times change, our stories evolve, but the stories of competition, conflict, conquest, and domination still shape our world today. However, these stories may drive us toward destruction if things continue in this way. In such a scenario, the story of humanity would become a tale of our species' most significant failure, despite our immense potential. Since nobody would listen to or learn from this story, it would be lost in the total oblivion of human history.

So, what should we do if the stories we tell ourselves, the stories we believe in and rely on, restrict us, bring pain to our lives, and contribute to the destruction of our world? Apart from the existing stories we inherit and pass on, are there other stories we could embrace?

We need new stories. We must find a fresh narrative that gives meaning and value to humanity's existence on Earth. We must create a story that fosters a sense of responsibility to create a world where all life can coexist harmoniously, beyond just the human species. While we have ancestral stories known as archetypes, we are still lacking shared stories about our future.

Creating new stories is both simple and challenging. Humans are natural-born storytellers, and our brains are wired for storytelling. Every day, we create stories and reshape existing ones. The real challenge lies not in creating stories but in embracing them as our own and genuinely believing in them. It's about weaving that narrative into our own lives.

Creating new stories starts with recognizing that our existing beliefs are stories. And because they are stories, they can change, allowing new narratives to emerge. This observation applies not only to personal beliefs but also to cultural traditions and religious convictions. It may be challenging for some individuals; they might feel anger when their beliefs are referred to as stories. Considering our beliefs as absolute truth while dismissing all others as mere fiction and falsehood, however, prevents coexistence. It is crucial to acknowledge that unless we transcend this perspective of dominance and destruction, we will remain trapped in a cycle of hostile confrontation and conflict.

If we truly open our minds, we can embrace differences in cultural and religious beliefs just as we appreciate variety in clothing styles or culinary traditions. These differences add richness to human culture and offer unique life experiences, and they should never be the reason for bloody battles and conflicts. Instead of clinging to our convictions as the absolute truth, we can approach them as personal or collective preferences while equally respecting the stories and beliefs of others.

Creating new stories doesn't mean throwing away the ones we already have; it involves reinterpreting and expanding their meanings. Take, for instance, a story that celebrates a tribe's prosperity through a tribal deity. We can reinterpret it to recognize that all of humanity is, in essence, one global tribe. In the same way, we can expand a story that suggests humans have the right to dominate the world. We can redefine *dominance* to mean our responsibility to create a peaceful and sustainable world where all beings coexist harmoniously.

Doing so allows us to breathe new life into our existing stories, making them more beautiful, profound, and complete. Our consciousness as a species has grown and evolved, and we are now open to embracing new narratives. On the contrary, old customs and belief systems are becoming obstacles to creating new stories as they fail to keep up with the changes in human awareness.

To pave the way for a new story of humanity, we must reflect and ask ourselves some important questions: What kind of beings do we want to become? What is the purpose and significance of our existence on Earth? What kind of world do we envision creating? Choosing a story for ourselves goes beyond rationality or convincing arguments; it requires us to tap into our empathy and feeling. Which story resonates more authentically with your heart: one of competition, conflict, domination, and destruction or one of empathy, solidarity, cooperation, and coexistence? Which story ignites hope and inspires you to the core?

The Scale of Our Stories

To create a new story that truly captures humanity's current state on Earth, one element we need to change is the scale of our perspective. In the past, stories primarily revolved around tribes or nations, with little consideration for values or ideals beyond our immediate community. That was the limit of the beliefs and imaginations of the storytellers. However, the world has changed. Our actions and interactions now transcend borders, and our impact on the environment is undeniable. Yet, our mindset remains anchored in outdated stories.

What does the Earth mean to us? Is it simply the place we find ourselves in, regardless of our intentions? Is it a mysterious and powerful force that inspires both fear and reverence? Is it a nurturing mother showing boundless love and patience despite our exploitation? Or is it a disposable resource to be used and discarded? None of these perspectives truly capture our present reality. Initially, the Earth served as the backdrop for humanity's struggle for survival, much like other creatures. As our capacity for symbolism and knowledge grew, nature became a source of wonder and awe. Most natural phenomena, such as the sea, forest, lightning, and wind, were attributed to deities. As knowledge and technology advanced and as we gained confidence in our abilities, nature became the subject of exploration and gradually became a target for exploitation.

Even during the industrial age, we mainly focused on the immediate effects of our actions on the environment and didn't give much thought to the broader global implications. People often brushed off discussions about climate issues as biased opinions. But things have taken a dramatic turn in recent years. Now, we're openly discussing the possibility of leaving Earth and seeking refuge on other planets because of the growing threats to our planet's livability.

The Earth is not just the backdrop to our lives. It is not a mystical force with unlimited power or a passive entity unaffected by our actions. The truth is we humans have a significant impact on the Earth. We can reshape landscapes, change climates, and even shape the destiny of our planet. But our mindset is still stuck in old stories, preventing us from fully embracing our roles and responsibilities. We need to rethink our relationship with the Earth to align with this reality. Perhaps the most suitable perspective is that of *management*. Instead of seeing ourselves as mere inhabitants, we should adopt an Earth management mindset.

What if we consider the Earth our own land, household, and business? What if we take on the responsibility of caring for, protecting, and managing it? If we approach the current state of the Earth with this mindset, how would it shape our choices and actions? When we start thinking of the Earth as a single connected entity, we realize we already have what it takes to restore ecological balance and ensure a sustainable future. We've got the principles, knowledge, technology, and resources at our disposal. The key lies in organizing and utilizing them collectively, driven by a shared purpose.

Our life's stage has expanded to encompass the entire Earth. It's time to broaden the scope of our story and to share the values it holds with the whole planet. The Earth needs responsible managers who consider the entire globe, not just their organization or country. We are the ones who can fulfill this role.

A New Paradigm Centered on Management

The relationship between humans and the Earth calls for a new paradigm. The old ways of fear, worship, possession, control, or exploitation don't work anymore. We truly need a mindset rooted in affection, responsible use, and protection—similar to how we care for our loved ones and our own homes or businesses. Houses and businesses can be rebuilt, but the Earth cannot, so it needs more careful and responsible use and protection. This paradigm shift from ownership and control to management and protection must form the framework for the new story of humanity and the planet.

From ownership and control to use and management

One significant business trend in the past decade is the rise of subscription services and sharing systems. Even after CDs and DVDs disappeared, many people still had music and videos as files on their computers or external hard drives. However, now most of us access streaming services through a membership fee, gaining access to a vast library surpassing our personal collections.

This model has expanded into various areas, from daily consumer goods to automobiles and houses. For instance, we use our vehicles for less than 10 percent of their ownership time, except for heavy equipment put into the work site. Many have realized that owning a car for that small fraction of usage is neither resource-efficient nor cost-effective. However, car-sharing hasn't become widespread due to the lack of real-time availability information and the influence of a culture that associates cars with wealth and success.

But things are changing. With the advancements in networks, information, and communication technology, real-time information on car availability is now accessible. As our lifestyles evolve, car-sharing has become a reality. And with the ongoing development of the Internet of Things and autonomous technology, the obsession with personal car ownership may become outdated.

A profound paradigm shift occurs underneath what may seem like a simple technological change. We're moving away from the traditional ideas of ownership and control and focusing on proper use and management. This shift is especially noticeable in sustainability, particularly in developing sustainable living environments such as housing, communities, and cities.

For example, efforts are being made in group housing to enhance the quality of life while reducing personal space costs by providing quality shared spaces. Moreover, in the future, we will design communities to create a seamless connection between living and working spaces, minimize car use, and balance privacy and community engagement.

If we are creative, we can extend the shift from owning and controlling to using and managing various aspects of our lives. Think about children's play equipment, storybooks, or textbooks that lose their relevance over time, interior items you'd like to switch based on the season, special clothes or accessories with limited use, and computers that require periodic upgrades to keep up with new technologies. Instead of owning these items, using and sharing them for a specific period is more advantageous.

This approach benefits not only individuals but also communities and the planet. Personal preferences, obsessions, and cultural traditions may hinder this change. However, if we highlight the ethical integrity associated with sustainability, showcasing its economic benefits, and framing these practices as innovative and trendy, we can overcome these hurdles.

Transitioning from competition to cooperation

We all know trust and cooperation bring more advantages than distrust and competition. Yet, we often find ourselves caught in a costly cycle of trying to figure out others' motives while concealing our own, constantly verifying information, and engaging in obstructive or attacking behaviors to protect ourselves in competitive situations. In highly competitive industries, it is not uncommon for some businesses to exit the market due to the inability to afford the costs of the chicken game, where they compete at the risk of destroying themselves until one side wins.

Recognizing the social costs of distrust, governments take extensive measures to build trust systems. They implement various strategies, such as credit rating systems, government payment guarantees, notarization and registration processes for large transactions, and strict penalties for bounced checks.

Especially in the recent experience of the pandemic, we've witnessed firsthand the critical need for trust, information sharing, and cooperation between countries. We've seen the devastating damage that occurs when trust breaks down and the remarkable effectiveness of preparedness that comes from trust.

We're confronting a crisis of unprecedented scale that cannot be resolved without trust and cooperation. This global crisis includes climate change, potential future pandemics, and the uncertain controllability of AI technologies. The technical conditions necessary for cooperation in these areas, such as reliable data and real-time updates, are already available. The challenge lies in building trust and cultivating the will to cooperate.

Thankfully, we possess the intelligence to discern what truly benefits us. The question is, how far can we expand our interests in terms of time and space? If we limit our thinking to just today, this month, or this year, collaboration might not seem all that appealing. It might not feel like a priority if future generations will only enjoy the benefits hundreds of years later.

However, considering our currently available information, the choices and actions we make today will impact us within the next five to ten years or even sooner. Whether raising children, building homes, or running businesses, we're accustomed to looking five to ten years ahead and making choices that will serve us best. It's simply a sensible judgment that any responsible parent or manager would make.

Therefore, we don't have to expect everyone to become enlightened sages overnight to shift the paradigm from competition to cooperation. Wise selfishness is enough. By making choices that benefit ourselves in the long run, we'll start witnessing the incredible impact of change. We'll begin to understand how we've become trapped in the paradigm we've created and see the immense pain, damage, and impoverishment it has brought to our lives, communities, and the entire ecosystem of our precious planet.

From development and exploitation to balance and recovery

The development field has always been a money-making venture. It covers various activities such as building cities, constructing housing complexes, establishing commercial districts, and tapping into underground resources like petroleum, iron ore, logging, and pastures. These endeavors have brought in substantial profits and contributed to economic growth.

However, finding balance and ensuring sustainability has become essential in all these areas. If development projects overlook these factors, they face many roadblocks, such as public opposition and government regulations, challenging long-term success.

In the coming years, one crucial focus that will gain increasing importance is *recovery*. It's about restoring damaged environments, ecosystems, and climate systems. This undertaking will be massive, perhaps one of the most significant projects in human history. Getting things back on track will require substantial physical and human resources and herculean effort.

Restoring something damaged to its original state is no easy feat. It takes much more time, energy, and dedication than the initial action that caused the damage. Considering its magnitude, this project also has the potential to generate a wealth of benefits. It will restore our environment and create numerous jobs, bring people together, and yield the most positive and enduring return on investment.

More and more people are realizing the urgency of recovery efforts. As we witness the growing hardships brought by the current state of the Earth, our awareness deepens. As a species, we have a remarkable track record of problem-solving, showcasing our creativity and ingenuity throughout history. Just think about how we've explored the ocean's depths, expanded our habitats, and even set foot on other planets. These abilities don't need to be used only for development or exploitation. Precisely the same skills can help us restore balance.

During the COVID-19 pandemic, something remarkable happened. Lockdown measures forced us to pause our social activities, and within a surprisingly short time, we witnessed meaningful environmental changes. The air quality improved noticeably, and we saw a resurgence of endangered animal and plant populations. These changes, enforced by circumstance, provide robust evidence of how our collective behavior can significantly impact the environment. Imagine what we could achieve if we took deliberate and systematic actions for restoration on a global scale. The potential impact is beyond our wildest imagination.

From profitability to sustainability

As awareness of climate change and the need for sustainability spreads, businesses realize the importance of eco-friendliness and sustainability in their operations and product development. Ignoring these considerations or going against sustainability practices is no longer viable in the market.

Sustainability has become a key consideration in marketing and promotion, but it's still lagging in cost analysis, profitability assessment, and business performance evaluation. Many people believe we should always consider sustainability despite potential cost increases and reduced profitability. However, they don't think sustainability alone can reduce costs and increase profits in the long run.

This situation exposes a significant flaw in our current market economy system. The impacts and footprints we leave on the Earth through economic activities, such as production and consumption, do not simply disappear. They come with actual costs that we will eventually bear, even if not immediately recognized. Unfortunately, the current market economy does not factor in these costs adequately.

We're already paying substantial prices for clean water. As people trust tap water less, they buy more bottled water, although most bottled water comes from the tap. It costs more than gasoline in many countries, even three times as much as in the United Sates. Now, imagine a world where we have to pay for the air we breathe, which is currently freely available.

How much would that cost us? The masks we wore during the COVID-19 pandemic and severe smog have given us a taste of that terrifying possibility.

What about the immeasurable value of the green spaces we've destroyed, the species we've driven to extinction, and the ecosystems we've pushed to the brink of collapse? For example, if rising sea temperatures disrupt the distribution of nutrients and the vital marine food chain, how much would it cost to restore it? Is it even possible to restore these systems, regardless of how much we're willing to pay?

The recovery of these massive systems can take hundreds of thousands or even millions of years, far beyond a mere decade or two. And yet, signs of crisis are already happening before our eyes. The bills for our actions are already in front of us, though we may not have realized it yet.

It would be impractical to expect individuals to bear these costs in their production and consumption choices voluntarily. This responsibility falls on the shoulders of the state and international organizations. Initiatives like greenhouse gas emission quotas and carbon taxes are moving us in the right direction. As this understanding becomes more widespread, we can honestly account for and pay the actual costs and prices of the goods and services we produce and consume. That's when sustainability will become an essential value that upholds profitability and aligns with our practical needs rather than a lofty moral burden that compromises profitability.

From success to completion

When we embrace this paradigm shift and align our personal goals with it, something remarkable takes place. It's a profound shift in our consciousness, thoughts, behavior, lifestyle, and even our culture. This personal transformation transcends the pursuit of success; it propels us toward a state of completion—an inner perfection that brings unparalleled fulfillment.

Success, tied to fierce competition, is inherently unattainable for everyone. It sets a goal out of reach for the majority. We see this vividly in highly competitive education systems like South Korea, where elementary school students attend specialized private academies to get into medical school. The actual acceptance rate for medical school is less than 1 percent of all university admissions. Can you imagine the intense competition these kids face, even before they reach age 10, where the majority are systematically determined to fall short?

The competition doesn't stop there, even if they make it into that 1 percent. Comparisons, evaluations, and further competition persist within that small group. If someone finds satisfaction and happiness along this path, it would be luck and a blessing rather than a natural outcome of success. In many societies today, the relentless pursuit of success often leads to stress and suffering instead of genuine happiness.

On the other hand, completion doesn't rely on external judgments. It's about recognizing and being satisfied with the values you hold dear and bringing them to life. As people reflect on their life's journey, especially toward the end, they often come to a profound realization: genuine happiness, comfort, and peace cannot be found in external achievements or the opinions of others. It comes from the recognition and contentment found within oneself.

When we achieve a goal, we often feel a sense of accomplishment, excitement, and pride. However, as time passes, these feelings may fade, and we begin to listen to our inner voice. We question ourselves: How do I feel? Am I genuinely happy and satisfied? If something feels missing or empty, we often realize that what we were pursuing may not have been what we truly wanted, prompting us to search for new goals. It could be a different job, a new degree, a life partner, or even a change in our overall circumstances. This cycle of setting external goals, striving for them, reflecting on our inner feelings, and seeking new aspirations can happen throughout our lives.

One thing becomes clear: ultimately, our inner feelings are the measure of fulfillment, not external accomplishments. That sense of completeness is what we've been searching for all along. Based on our personal experiences and the stories of many others, we know that this feeling of fulfillment comes from internal qualities such as kindness, service, dedication, responsibility, integrity, courage, and authenticity. Pursuing these values of completion doesn't require competition. In fact, when we all adopt these values, we can support and uplift one another without taking away opportunities from others.

There is no conflict between pursuing inner completion and striving for external goals. It's simply a matter of setting priorities. Since the COVID-19 pandemic, our world has changed rapidly, increasing uncertainty and anxiety. As a result, mental health has become a pressing global concern. Society increasingly recognizes the importance of individuals with strong minds, ethical character, and trustworthiness.

We're witnessing a cultural shift where virtues like authenticity and integrity are gaining greater appreciation. These shifts create new opportunities for success by emphasizing inner fulfillment and nurturing strong personal values. If we aim for completion and accept success as a gift, we can lead a fulfilling and rewarding life. We live in an era where such possibilities are becoming increasingly attainable.

A True Hero of Our Time

In our story, alongside the new paradigm, there is another crucial element: the hero. We all love a good hero, don't we? They've been at the heart of countless stories passed down through generations. These tales may have different characters with diverse backgrounds but they share a common thread.

These stories always have a villain to be feared, and the hero's journey is about facing and conquering these challenges with unwavering determination and courage. They go through ups and downs, but ultimately, they triumph and protect or achieve something significant. Whether it's in ancient myths or modern sci-fi movies, we can't help but get drawn into these stories and cheer for the hero.

But what truly makes them heroes? It's not just their physical strength or exceptional combat skills, as many villains also possess those qualities. The essential characteristic of a hero is their selfless-ness, their willingness to give everything for the sake of others without considering their interests. This quality of heroes often goes unnoticed because we are dazzled by their bravery and impressive feats. But, their true strength lies in their capacity to love.

Why do stories with familiar themes, told repeat-edly throughout history, still grab our attention? It's because they create a particular resonance within us and evoke emotions that we enjoy. If these stories didn't strike a chord or if we didn't like the feelings they stirred, they wouldn't have stood the test of time and continued to be passed down through generations.

When we witness a human being who fights for a cause greater than themselves and overcomes seem-ingly impossible odds, something inside us responds and resonates. At this moment, it's not just the hero's outer appearance that captures our attention. The hero's inner strength and human greatness shine through their actions and character. We truly see the reflection of our human nature, recognizing and resonating with that greatness. The hero we applaud and admire is, in fact, a reflection of ourselves.

Right now, humanity is confronting a crisis unlike any we've seen before. It's a crisis that impacts the very survival of our species. This isn't just a local or regional problem; it's a global crossroads we find ourselves in. In fact, it's the first time since modern humans appeared 300,000 years ago that we're facing such a massive global crisis. Crises give rise to heroes, and heroes emerge from crises. These challenging times have a way of awakening the greatness within us. The Earth and all its living beings are sending us urgent messages, calling for us to wake up and step up. It's time to take action and make a difference.

Our time needs heroes who take on the responsibility of preserving and protecting our planet. The Earth is in desperate need of these heroes. Our challenges are enormous, and they call for a collective effort. We don't just need one or two heroes. We need a whole army of them. Together, we can rise to the occasion and become the heroes our world desperately needs.

The Great Story of Humanity That Has Yet to Begin

When we think about our lives, organizations, and nations, 300,000 years (the time of modern humans on Earth) sounds like a long time. But it's quite short in the grand scheme of Earth's history. Consider that dinosaurs ruled the planet for a staggering 150 million years before humans came into the picture. And even before the dinosaurs, bacteria and fungi were already here, enduring multiple mass extinctions and shaping life for billions of years.

For most of our history, humans were not dominant in harsh environments. We lived in fear, constantly hiding and being hunted. In only the last few tens of thousands of years, we gained an advantage over other species. And it was only a few hundred years ago that we started taking charge, shaping, and conquering the natural world.

In the last few hundred years, many of the problems humans have created could be seen as unintended consequences of not fully understanding our abilities and potential. It's like in superhero movies, where the hero suddenly discovers their power but doesn't know how to control it. They end up causing chaos, destroying things, and scaring people unintentionally. It's a period of confusion where they're still figuring out who they want to be and their role. But eventually, they learn to harness their power for good, making choices that help others. That's when a true superhero is born.

Who are we? What kind of beings does humanity want to become? What is the meaning and value of our existence on Earth? On a personal level, we may be used to questioning our identities and desires. But so far, asking these questions about humanity has been left to the intellectuals. Until now, human civilization has been too self-centered and preoccupied with its concerns to confront these profound questions genuinely. As a result, we have yet to find the answers.

This fact means humanity's greatest story is still waiting to be written. It can be a short and tragic tale, fading into oblivion with no one to listen. Or it could be a magnificent saga of discovery, growth, and creation that spans thousands of years, something like the following:

In the 21st century, Earth finds itself on the precipice of a profound crisis. Desperate for a glimmer of hope, the planet yearns for individuals with the untapped potential to recognize their true worth and rescue it from impending doom. Just as all seems lost, an extraordinary phenomenon occurs.

Across the globe, many people awaken to a newfound consciousness, embracing the profound responsibility to safeguard themselves and protect all life on Earth. United by a shared vision, they dedicate themselves to creating a world that thrives in peace and sustains harmony.

Their collective efforts produce a seismic shift, steering Earth away from the brink of catastrophe. As this awakening reverberates like an explosive wave, the planet regains equilibrium, ushering in an era where all coexist harmoniously in a peaceful and sustainable world. Humanity, at long last, builds an enlightened civilization founded on the timeless value of coexistence.

No one is forcing us to follow this path, nor is it pre-determined by any supernatural design. It is a story we create together, shaping our values and giving meaning to our lives. When we adopt this narrative, everything starts to change. We think, feel, and act differently. The story becomes enriched through shared experiences and connections, shaping our lifestyle, culture, and ultimately, a new civilization.

If this is the story of humanity, then the pain the Earth is currently experiencing will be a valuable labor for the birth of a new humanity.

CHAPTER 3

Who Do We Want to Be?

Who will form the new humanity, set to complete the unwritten human story, a story both beautiful and profound? They are individuals who recognize the Earth's urgent need for change and embrace their power to enact it. These are the souls who understand that shifts in consciousness, thought, and action must happen together—swiftly and globally. They grasp that not just a few, but millions—even tens of millions—of people will shape the planet's fate through voluntary awakening and collective choice. These are the minds who firmly believe in humanity's inherent determination, passion, and wisdom to embark on this journey.

Who is this new humanity, and what makes it different? The new humanity believes in the ability to choose its own identity and takes pride in being an Earth Citizen. They recognize that they are part of nature and willingly take responsibility for the planet's future. These beliefs form the foundation of their values, guide their actions, and create a bond of solidarity among them. By adopting and living out these beliefs, the new humanity can attain coexistence and write stories of discovery, growth, and creation that will endure for generations to come.

We Choose Who We Are

We recognize that we are not bound by any dogma, religion, or limiting belief system. By breaking free from the constraints of the past, we take ownership of our bodies, minds, and consciousness and create a new path toward a more peaceful and sustainable future.

The "Who am I?" question may seem simple but is often unfamiliar to many of us. When we take a moment to reflect and ask ourselves this question, we might realize that a significant portion of our answers come from external sources—the environment we grew up in and the circumstances that shaped us from birth.

Unless we've led an exceptionally different life, most of our basic information, such as name, race, family background, place of birth, appearance, skin color, and language, is determined from the moment we enter the world. We tend to accept these answers without much thought or questioning. That's why the question "Who am I?" is something people don't usually ask themselves in their everyday lives unless they're going through a period of deep reflection or engaging in specific spiritual practices.

Most of the time, we are not the ones that ask the question, "Who am I?" It's usually other people who are curious to know about us. We tend to live our lives without really delving into that question ourselves. As a result, the question of our identity loses its significance because we don't have a say in it and cannot choose or change it.

Most of us take our given identity for granted and let it shape our lives. Factors like our country, ethnicity, religion, and ideologies have a powerfully divisive impact on how we think, feel, and act. These divisions based on information can create barriers, even between people who speak the same language and drink from the same river. People with no personal grudges can become enemies and even shed blood just because of these differences.

The information that shapes our identities can get in the way of uniting and collaborating to tackle the global crisis we face. That's why a new humanity starts by freeing ourselves from the constraints of identity information that hold us back, particularly the dogmatic types of information.

But letting go of these constraints doesn't mean we throw them away altogether. They're still valuable life experiences that teach important lessons for our future choices. It means not allowing this information to limit our thoughts and actions. We need to break free from the narrow boundaries it imposes on us. By doing so, we open ourselves up to a clearer understanding of what's truly needed in the present moment, enabling us to make choices and take actions free from pre-conceived notions and prejudices.

Another form of information that restricts our choices and actions is self-imposed limitations. Take a moment and ask yourself, "What kind of person am I?" Jot down the answers that come to your mind. Which answers empower you, and which hold you back? How honestly do those answers reflect yourself?

Now, ask yourself another question: "How do I want to be remembered when my life ends?" Take a moment to ponder this question and reflect on your answer. Chances are, your response reflects your wish to be remembered as someone who has made a difference by helping others and positively impacting the world. It's innate within us to have this desire and inclination to assist others and contribute in meaningful ways. It speaks to the core of our human nature and our inherent goodness.

Are you worried about the future of humanity and our planet? Do you have a strong desire to contribute and positively address the challenges we're facing? Most likely, your answer to these questions is a resounding, "Yes!" And you're not alone.

When I asked this question to numerous individuals, the overwhelming majority responded similarly. It's truly remarkable. Throughout history, few ordinary people have been genuinely concerned about the well-being of humanity and our planet. Advancements in culture or education systems don't drive this extraordinary change we're witnessing. This deep-seated mindset has always existed within us and is now being awakened by the pressing global challenges and crises we encounter.

There's a belief that individuals are naturally selfish and that we're powerless to make a difference in the world. That belief couldn't be further from the truth. Deep within every heart, there exists a noble desire to help others and leave a positive impact on the world. It's part of our true nature as human beings. In today's world, we need awareness and action from each of us. We can't just sit back and think that someone else will handle our problems.

The first step is to let go of the limited information that has defined us thus far. We are so much more than the labels and boundaries that society and ourselves have placed upon us. We need to acknowledge and embrace the vast, bright consciousness that resides within us as our true essence.

This process is like a new birth, where we liberate ourselves from the dogmatic information that defines us and break free from the limiting beliefs that hinder our progress. While physical birth establishes our existence, this birth establishes our true worth. It's about choosing who we truly are and giving birth to our own being. It's not about the mother giving birth to us but rather about our consciousness giving birth to ourselves. And the beauty of it is that age or gender doesn't matter. It's a transformative journey that anyone can undertake, regardless of circumstances.

When we free ourselves from limiting beliefs and information, we become masters of our bodies and minds. We tap into our brains' full power and realize our greatest potential. Previously, we may have thought and acted as separate, self-centered, and helpless individuals tied to a specific race, religion,

A New Humanity

ethnicity, or group. But now, freed from the confines of such information, we can become thoughtful individuals, aware of our presence on Earth at this critical juncture. As mature and responsible individuals, we can assess, choose, and take action independently. We can confidently declare, "I choose, and I act." Our bodies and minds are tools we can harness to make a positive impact. We bring forth the best of our abilities by making choices that benefit the entire global community. Together, we forge a sustainable future for all of humanity.

We Are Earth Citizens

We recognize that we are citizens of the world, transcending skin color, language, race, culture, religion, and nationality. We understand that we share a common identity as inhabitants of this planet. We are committed to fostering the health of the Earth and all life and to promoting harmonious coexistence with each other and the Earth.

We draw information from various sources to define and understand ourselves, including aspects like skin color, language, race, religion, and nationality. Yet, what unites us all before these differences is our connection to Earth. We are Earth Citizens first and foremost before we call ourselves Americans, Koreans, Chinese, or French, or Asian, European, or African. We are Earth Citizens before identifying as Christians, Buddhists, Muslims, or Jews. The Earth Citizen identity is more fundamental than all others.

We naturally embrace our Earth citizenship when we break free from rigid beliefs and ideologies. It's like peeling away all those artificial layers, revealing our true identity as Earth Citizens, which is inherent to us. Becoming an Earth Citizen doesn't require any special training or preparation. When we realize that our old self-identity and the beliefs that once defined us no longer match our current situation, we need to choose to shed those old layers, just like a growing child must give up baby clothes that no longer fit.

We've overlooked the self-evident truth of our Earth citizenship for far too long. We've confined ourselves within the borders of nations, ethnicities, religions, and ideologies, often excluding or destroying those with different beliefs or identities.

By embracing our natural and shared identity as Earth Citizens, we can see others for who they truly are beyond artificial divisions. This viewpoint allows us to form genuine connections as fellow human beings. Recognizing our interconnectedness, we choose coexistence and work together to safeguard one another, taking collective responsibility for a sustainable future on Earth.

Once we wholeheartedly embrace our Earth citizenship, differences cease to be sources of conflict. Instead, cultural, racial, religious, and belief diversity is celebrated as a coexisting richness, contributing to a more inclusive human culture.

Moreover, being an Earth Citizen extends beyond the scope of Earth itself. Once we venture beyond our planet, much of the defining information that holds significance on Earth becomes less relevant, just as when we travel to other countries, our nationality matters more than specific cities or towns. Similarly, our fundamental identity as Earth Citizens remains unchanged regardless of humanity's future activities beyond Earth. Embracing this fact becomes even more crucial as we explore further into the universe. We have always been Earth Citizens, and that identity will persist. We cherish and take pride in being Earth Citizens, loving and respecting our home planet.

We Are Nature

We recognize that we are not separate from nature but an integral part of it. We understand that our actions have a profound impact on the natural world. By embracing our natural essence, we restore our connection with nature and work toward creating a healthier relationship with our planet.

What does nature mean to us? Is it a source of awe and joy, or is it merely seen as a resource to be exploited and discarded after serving its purpose? Throughout history, cultures once revered nature, but over time, this perception shifted toward conquest and utilization, particularly with the rise of industrialization. Despite evolving attitudes, the core notion of nature being separate from humans remains unaltered.

We are not outside of nature; we are part of nature. We stand firmly on the ground, deeply connected to the natural world. As we drink the water that circulates the Earth, we actively participate in the hydrologic cycle of this planet. Breathing the same air as all the animals and plants, we are intertwined with the very essence of life on our planet.

Our connection with nature goes far beyond picturesque landscapes. It's in the very essence of our being. Our bodies constantly function without our conscious control. At this very moment, our bodies are in constant motion. Cells are continually being created and dying while our hearts beat tirelessly to keep blood circulating throughout our entire body, keeping us alive and well. The sensory information from our surroundings ceaselessly flows into our brains, shaping our perception of the world. All of this occurs independently of our will or control.

We didn't consciously acquire our bodily functions and don't fully understand how they work. Most of the time, we only notice them when something goes wrong, like feeling pain. Our lives tend to focus on our interests and desires, making us believe we're in complete control. But the truth is, many crucial aspects of our well-being happen automatically, beyond our conscious influence. Nature takes the lead in keeping us alive. The statement that we are nature is not merely a poetic metaphor; it's a clear and undeniable fact.

Realizing that we are nature itself, not separate from it, allows us to understand our deep connection with all other living beings. Many traditional cultures and spiritual teachings expressed this interconnectedness as a vast net or tapestry.

Nature is not something to fear or conquer; it's not just an environment handed to us. We are nature; it is an inseparable part of our being. Our lives are interconnected with the grand life of the Earth. Accepting this reality will lead us to acknowledge the true value of healthy soils, clean water, and fresh air. Only then will we be willing to pay the rightful price to preserve and protect these essential elements. The urgency of prioritizing a sustainable planet will outweigh the allure of short-term gains and conveniences. We will begin to perceive cooperating in creating a sustainable future as more natural than striving for competition and success.

We Are the Earth's Future

We recognize that the Earth's future is not someone else's problem but the responsibility of each of us to protect and preserve. By embracing this responsibility, we can create a sustainable and thriving future for our planet and all its residents.

This era is a special time on Earth, and we are in a crucial position to determine its fate. One undeniable truth stands: we cannot evade this role and responsibility, whether we participate actively or stand by passively. It is a role bestowed upon each of us living on Earth now; it is our destined purpose.

Many people still view climate change as a distant future risk. Discussions often focus on the future of the Earth or generations yet to come. This perspective inadvertently hampers urgent action. Consider how you feel about ancestors from five or six generations ago; there's often a sense of detachment from them. When you have young grandchildren, their well-being becomes a priority, and you hold them close to your heart. Yet, it's more challenging to feel the same level of concern for descendants four or five generations ahead. Few people can naturally extend their care and consideration to such distant descendants, which might hinder the urgency of addressing climate change.

The future we face regarding climate change is not distant; it is imminent. According to the latest IPCC report, within the next 10 to 30 years, climate change trends will determine the consequences. Current projections suggest a 1.5-degree temperature rise by the 2030s and a 2.0-degree rise by 2050, resulting in far more significant and devastating impacts than we currently witness.

Given the average life expectancy in the United States is almost 80 years, the majority of individuals under 50, if we don't make drastic changes, will directly experience the catastrophic consequences of climate change within their lifetime. This reality applies to the United States and most people worldwide. The future we contemplate in the context of climate change is not about future generations; it is about ourselves and our families.

What choice would you make in this situation? Many individuals still believe that the Earth is too vast and that individual efforts won't significantly impact its future. They might rely on governments, large companies, or international organizations to handle the issue. Some people with strong religious beliefs may accept everything as God's will and focus on their spiritual salvation rather than the Earth's material continuity. Others might think that if climate change and environmental disasters ruin the Earth, it wouldn't be unfair, and they wouldn't complain since everyone will eventually die.

However, we hold the power to shape the planet's future, and there is still time to take action. The global temperature has risen significantly over the past few hundred years since industrialization began.

Scientists widely agree that human activity is the primary cause of current climate change. If we can make this mess, we also have the power to fix it. There has been extensive research and discussions on climate change, and we have plenty of solutions to tackle this problem.

The real question is, *who will take action*? It's not about relying on gods, political leaders, entrepreneurs, or scientists. It's up to each one of us—we are the ones who hold the responsibility. Depending on where you live, you might feel the crisis differently, but the truth is climate change and environmental disasters impact every corner of the world. It's a global issue that demands collective effort. Regardless of age or location, we must all be engaged and proactive in reducing its impact and preventing catastrophic consequences.

It's not just a metaphor; we are genuinely the future of the Earth. Depending on our choices and actions, humanity may have a future or none. Each of us living in this special time on Earth right now doesn't simply impact the future of the Earth; we are the future of the Earth. New humanity understands this truth and embraces the collective responsibility of safeguarding the Earth's future.

* * * * *

I choose who I am; my fundamental identity is that of an Earth Citizen. I am not separate from nature but an integral part of it. My thoughts, choices, and actions today will shape the future of the Earth that I will experience firsthand. This is the declaration of the new humanity.

Despite being something most people would readily agree with, it hasn't fully blossomed into a universal identity and lifestyle for all of humanity. For the self-declaration of the new humanity to transform from a mere piece of information into a belief and a way of life, it's essential to awaken a consciousness that translates into concrete actions. It's not our career, qualifications, or social status that define us as part of the new humanity. Nor is it reflected in a photo or profile on social media.

The spark for becoming part of the new humanity doesn't come from external factors; it's ignited by an inner realization: "We can't go on living like this. If we continue with the same thoughts and actions as before, the Earth and mankind will have no hope. I need to change, starting with myself." It's this awakening within us that shapes the new humanity we aspire to be.

CHAPTER 4

What Can We Do Now?

The challenges our planet faces right now are urgent and real, happening right before us. As part of the new humanity committed to a sustainable future for Earth, what steps should we take at this moment? Here are five immediate response actions and change guidelines for individuals to practice in their daily lives.

First, we must maintain our body's natural health and practice self-care. Second, adopting lifestyles that foster harmony and balance with nature is crucial. Third, we need to nurture a culture of peace and coexistence. Fourth, responsible technology use and support for sustainable development are vital. Lastly, we need to educate ourselves and others about the need for change and how we can make a positive impact. By taking these actions and encouraging others to do the same, we can create a harmonious and sustainable future for the planet and all life on it.

Nurturing Natural Health and Self-Care

We care for our own physical, mental, and emotional wellness naturally and proactively whenever possible and help others do the same.

In our society today, staying healthy has become a costly affair. Many of us believe that maintaining good health requires expensive high-tech equipment, facilities, and the help of experts. However, the recent pandemic has shown how vulnerable these systems we depend on are.

Our bodies are incredible at maintaining a healthy balance and healing when things go wrong. This ability isn't just limited to humans; all animals and plants have it too. From childhood, we've seen how wounds heal, bruises fade away, and muscles recover over time. Even when we catch a cold and feel terrible, our bodies work hard to get us back on our feet within a few days. It's all thanks to the natural healing power within us. Of course, this healing power does have its limits. If the damage is too severe, our bodies may not fully recover; in some cases, it can even be life-threatening. But no matter the circumstances, our bodies always do their best to restore balance and keep us going.

As medicine advances, we often rely on medications and doctors even for minor health concerns, thinking they cure our illnesses. However, the truth is that all treatments work by harnessing our body's natural healing abilities. Whether it's through drugs, electromagnetic waves, or surgery, medical therapies create the needed environment for healing to take place. Ultimately, our body's innate healing ability drives recovery, a power that has always been vital and continues to be essential today. Without this natural healing function, any treatment would eventually prove ineffective.

Our pursuit of natural health doesn't mean rejecting medical treatment or solely relying on natural remedies to cure diseases. Instead, it's about creating and maintaining optimal conditions for our body to restore its original balance in any situation. By prioritizing natural health, our body and mind become more resilient to various stresses, making it harder to get sick in the first place. And even if we do fall ill, we can often recover with minimal medical assistance. Suppose more people had this natural resilience—we could significantly reduce the demand for expensive medical equipment, drugs, and services. This, in turn, would help address the increasing medical expenses faced by countries worldwide, regardless of their economic development level.

Natural health benefits us and plays a vital role in keeping the environment healthy. When we take medicines, many chemicals they contain do not decompose naturally and can persist in the environment for a long time. Once these chemical substances have served their purpose in our bodies, they get discharged into sewage systems and rivers and eventually flow into the ocean. From there, they may be absorbed by marine life and travel up the food chain.

It's not just medications; the antibiotics used on livestock and other animals and pesticides on plants follow this cycle, too. By prioritizing natural health and using more natural remedies, we can reduce the amount of harmful chemicals entering the environment. Taking care of animals and plants, including ourselves, naturally and sustainably benefits our well-being and the natural environment.

Natural health also acts as a shield, safeguarding us from the impact of unexpected changes in our lives or surroundings. The recent pandemic highlighted the significance of personal resilience. When exposed to the same virus and experiencing similar symptoms, some people recover while others do not. The same applies to psychological trauma, where some individuals can handle considerable stress, but others may struggle even with minor pressure.

In a world where unexpected changes and shocks can shake our lives' foundations, strong internal resilience is essential for coping with these challenges. Imagine if a drug or medical service we rely on becomes unavailable, even temporarily or long-term. It can be quite unsettling. Thus, pursuing natural health and nurturing our body's healing power is crucial. It's a practical and essential practice that benefits us and those around us.

Three lifestyle habits that support natural health

Three simple yet powerful practices can improve natural health and benefit everyone: focused breathing, maintaining gut health, and mindful eating.

Breathing is something we all do without thinking much about it. But did you know it's like a master key for our well-being? It helps regulate our stress response, restores balance in our nervous system, and even supports our body's natural healing abilities. Our autonomic nervous system has two sides: the sympathetic nervous system, which triggers the stress response, and the parasympathetic nervous system, which induces relaxation. These days, many of us are constantly activating the sympathetic system by exposing ourselves to negative information and thoughts, creating our own stress. The problem is that when the sympathetic nervous system is in overdrive, the parasympathetic nervous system, responsible for digestion, rest, and recovery, gets suppressed. This means our body's natural healing power can't work as effectively.

Breathing is a simple and effective way to balance your nervous system. Taking just 3–4 deep, relaxed breaths can calm the overactive sympathetic nervous system and let the parasympathetic nervous system bring relaxation. There's a powerful natural healing system inside you, and your breath can supercharge it.

Prioritizing the health of your gut is another effective method to promote your overall well-being and sustain your physical and mental resilience. The gut is not just about digestion. It's a remarkable place with a neural network of around 300 to 500 million nerve cells. The gut also plays a crucial role in producing essential neurohormones like dopamine and serotonin, which affect our mood and happiness. At the same time, around 80 percent of our body's immune system is hard at work inside the gut, thanks to the diverse community of microbes.

To maintain a healthy gut condition, consider incorporating these methods. Enjoy the goodness of fermented vegetables like kimchi or sauerkraut. They're loaded with beneficial probiotics that support your gut health. Engage in exercises directly stimulating your intestines, such as *Abdominal Tapping*, where you rhythmically tap your lower abdomen with your palms or lightly clenched fists. Another one called *Intestinal Exercise* involves repeatedly pulling your belly in as much as possible and then releasing it. Start with 20–30 reps and gradually work up to 100 at a time, and repeat 3 times a day for both exercises. And don't forget gentle belly massage. Use your palms to give your lower abdomen some tender care.

Making a personal change to our eating habits can profoundly impact our health and the global environment. Though there's no perfect diet for everyone, we can follow some key guidelines that benefit us and the planet. One crucial step is reducing meat consumption, particularly red meat like beef. This small change can significantly reduce deforestation for pasture development and lower harmful methane gas emissions. Embracing a diet rich in various natural fiber-filled vegetables is an excellent alternative. Not only does it promote our individual health, but it also has a positive ripple effect on the entire planet.

Changing the type of food we eat is crucial, but it's equally vital to be mindful of the quantity. Overeating, no matter how healthy the food, can be harmful. So, find balance in your portions, and eat with a happy and grateful heart. It might sound like common sense, but it's powerful wisdom—choose nourishing foods, but don't stress over it. If healthy eating becomes a burden, it loses its positive impact. The key is to enjoy the process and not let it become a source of anxiety. And here's an essential reminder: approach your meals with gratitude and happiness. Avoid adding mental toxins through irritation or complaining, no matter the food's type or quality. Instead, eat with joy and appreciation for all the people and lives who have contributed to bringing that food to your table.

Energy meditation for self-care and connection

Energy meditation is another great practice I want to recommend for natural health and self-care. Modern physics has shown that we find energy when we break matter down into its smallest components. Specifically, it's a vibrating energy field influenced by consciousness or the mind. In East Asia's spiritual and academic traditions, it's believed that the mind and energy are two fundamental elements of the world, and they work together to bring about all changes.

Based on this understanding, they've developed mind-body training methods that explore awakening a sense of energy and using the power of the mind to create change. Generally, there are two approaches. One focuses on studying the mind, centered on scriptures and meditation. The other approach centers on the study of energy, which includes practices like martial arts and energy healing—commonly known as qigong.

However, since they started with the understanding that the mind and energy are not separate, we can learn how to use energy by understanding how the mind works through its study. Likewise, as we learn to move energy, we realize that it's our mind in action. The study of the mind intertwines with the study of energy, and vice versa.

Qigong starts with the simple act of feeling energy. It's all around us—inside and outside our bodies. There is this vast energy presence in the apparent void that seems completely empty, where darkness and silence reign between galaxies. To experience this energy, we begin by focusing our minds. As we concentrate, our senses become remarkably sharp, tuned in to the subtle energy flow.

Let's try energy meditation in this order:

Begin by clapping your hands about 30 times. After clapping, keep your palms open and concentrate on them for about 10 seconds. If your senses are well developed, and your mind is focused, you may experience a unique tingling electric sensation or a gentle sensation of magnetic currents.

Now clap your hands again about 30 times, then vigorously rub your palms together for 20–30 seconds until they become hot. Stop the movement, open your hands, and concentrate on the feeling in your palms for about 10 seconds. This time, you may notice the sensation of energy even more than the first time.

Shake your hands up and down quickly for 20–30 seconds, then stop and focus on the feeling in your palms for about 10 seconds with your hands open. In this state, gently close your eyes and slowly open and close your hands repeatedly without letting them touch. As you repeat the movement, pay attention to both palms and the sensation of the space between them. You might notice various sensations, such as the feeling of pushing something between your hands, the sense of them pulling toward each other, and a tingling electric current coursing through your palms. While keeping the feeling steady, open your arms wider to increase the distance between your hands. If the sense of energy weakens or disappears, close the gap again to revive the sensation.

Once you've established the sensation of energy even when your hands are apart, you can now move them freely, guided by the feeling of energy. As you do so, you'll notice that the distinction between the energy propelling the hand's movement, the moving hand, and the mind observing the movement dissolves. The separation between a subject that moves and an object that is moved fades away. Your mind, which experiences and observes all of this, simply exists without judgment, without emotions, and without boundaries. It becomes a pure state of being, fully present in the moment.

In this state, gently bring your hands together in front of your chest, like a prayer posture, and focus on the sensation in your chest. You may experience feelings of fullness, joy, and happiness beyond explanation. You might sense something akin to a bright light even with your eyes closed. Keep your attention focused as you slowly lower your hands to your knees, ensuring the feeling remains present.

Take three slow, deliberate breaths, inhaling and exhaling mindfully. On the final exhale, lower your head slightly to release any lingering tension in your neck or shoulders with your breath.

Now, open your eyes and rub your hands together, sweeping them across your head, face, neck, shoulders, chest, arms, legs, knees, and feet. This process energizes your entire body, leaving you feeling refreshed and revitalized. If you approach this practice with sincerity and focus, you can experience all this in just one attempt.

One of the most effective and practical ways to utilize energy is for healing. After completing the earlier procedure, rest one hand on your lap with the palm facing up. Gently bring the other hand closer to the uncomfortable part of your body, maintaining a distance of about one inch without touching your body. Let go of any thoughts, including the intention to heal, and focus your mind on the area that needs healing. Breathe comfortably while holding the feeling of energy in your hands.

By following this practice, your entire body, especially your hands, will become more awake, enabling you to sense the energy moving in and out. As you focus your mind, the energy naturally flows to the area that requires healing. This simple yet powerful process embodies the essence of qigong. It awakens your energy awareness and channels it to the intended target through concentrated attention. While you can learn more advanced techniques for harnessing energy, the fundamental principle remains the same. It's all about connecting with the energy within and directing it to where it's needed, fostering healing and balance.

Once you become familiar with this practice, you can apply it to various parts of your body and even share the energy with others. Awaken your hand's energy, focus your mind, bring your hand close to the area needing healing in another person, and transmit the energy as before. This process allows you to direct the healing energy precisely where required, both for yourself and those you wish to help.

With the power of your mind, energy meditation can extend beyond yourself or those close to you. You can direct healing energy to anyone or anything you focus on. One person can send energy to many, and vice versa. Time and distance are no obstacles; you can send comforting energy to someone far away or channel it toward achieving your goals. Moreover, the scope of this practice is limitless. You can send blessings and healing energy to the Earth, all living beings, and everything that exists.

Our mind knows no bounds—it can be infinitely expansive or infinitely focused. Likewise, the energy that moves our minds is boundless. The potential energy we can harness depends on the vastness of our minds. What do you truly desire? How much energy and focus are you willing to invest in it?

When many people align their thoughts and feelings, the power multiplies exponentially. With millions of individuals united by shared dreams and hopes, the vibrations and resonance of this collective energy exceed imagination.

By envisioning a peaceful world and healthy Earth, fueling that dream with hope and excitement, and taking action—big or small—we generate transformative energy capable of healing the planet. The ultimate qigong lies in the unified healing power of Earth Citizens coming together for the greater good of our shared home.

The natural health methods shared here, including breathing, gut health exercises, mindful eating, and energy meditation, are accessible to everyone. You don't need experts or to wait for changes in the medical system or policies. Right now, you have the power to start practicing and nurturing your well-being.

PRACTICE GUIDELINES FOR NATURAL HEALTH AND SELF-CARE

Exercise regularly: Engage in enjoyable physical activities like walking, jogging, swimming, yoga, or tai chi for at least 30 minutes most days. Include gut-health exercises like Intestinal Exercise and Abdominal Tapping.

Eat a balanced diet: Eat various fruits, vegetables, whole grains, lean proteins, and healthy fats. Be mindful of portion sizes and limit processed foods, sugar, red meat, and excessive caffeine or alcohol.

Prioritize sleep: Aim for 7–9 hours of quality sleep each night. Establish a consistent sleep schedule and create a soothing bedtime routine.

Practice mindfulness: Cultivate mindfulness or meditation regularly. Regularly engage in focused breathing and energy meditation.

Manage stress: Develop stress-management techniques like exercise, meditation, journaling, hobbies, or music. Identify stress triggers and find healthy coping mechanisms.

Seek social connections: Foster meaningful relationships and connect with others through clubs, volunteering, or group activities.

Spend time in nature: Connect with nature outdoors, walking, hiking, or simply observing its beauty.

Living in Harmony with Nature

We live in harmony with nature by reducing our carbon footprint, conserving energy and water, and protecting natural habitats and biodiversity.

Unless we're floating objects in the air, we all need space on land or in the ocean to survive. You need enough room for your two soles to stand, your hips and soles to sit, and your whole body length to lie down. For a basic standard of living, you need a room for a bed, a kitchen to cook, and a bathroom. It's not just about personal space. To produce everything we need to survive and live comfortably, we require even more land—farmland for crops, pastures for livestock, forests for timber, fishing grounds for fish, and space for factories to make goods.

The ecological footprint is a comprehensive measure of our impact on the environment. It takes into account various factors such as consuming natural spaces, disrupting animal habitats, diminishing species diversity, and emitting carbon dioxide. Currently, our ecological footprint is calculated to be 1.75 times Earth's available resources, given the current world population. However, the situation becomes even more alarming as countries like China and India strive to reach the consumption levels of developed nations, potentially increasing our footprint by over five times the Earth's size! What will happen when our footprint outgrows the Earth's capacity to sustain it on such a massive scale?

Reducing your carbon footprint

The carbon footprint is a key aspect of the ecological footprint, focusing specifically on how much carbon dioxide we release into the air through human activities. It has significantly increased since industrialization and is a major cause of current climate change. In 2015, representatives from 196 countries attended an environmental summit in Paris, France, and reached a meaningful agreement to address this issue. However, the agreement faced setbacks as major countries, like the United States and China, among the largest carbon dioxide emitters, didn't fully comply and even withdrew from it.

Global atmospheric carbon dioxide concentrations surpassed 400 ppm in 2013 and currently stand at 420 ppm. Earth's climate has experienced natural fluctuations throughout its history, with periods of rising and falling temperatures. There were times when carbon dioxide levels and atmospheric temperatures were higher than they are today. However, the critical difference now is the speed of change. In the past, such changes occurred gradually over thousands or tens of thousands of years. But after industrialization, we've witnessed significant changes in just a few hundred years.

Based on fossil records, about 3 million years ago, Earth's atmosphere had similar carbon dioxide levels as today. Back then, the temperature was approximately 2 to 3 degrees higher than before industrial times. This means that even if we magically achieved zero carbon emissions right now, the CO_2 already in the atmosphere would still push the temperature well beyond the desired 1.5 degrees. If we act fast and cut carbon emissions to zero as soon as we can and work hand-in-hand with nature's carbon absorption systems like forests, land, and oceans, we can at least slow down the runaway temperature rise. If we fail to act swiftly and let the temperature hit that dreaded 2-degree mark, things will spiral out of control. Chain effects will kick in, making it nearly impossible to keep the temperature from surpassing 6 degrees. Such a catastrophic scenario could lead to a mass extinction event.

Why is it so challenging to reduce carbon dioxide emissions? Because it's an integral part of our daily existence. Carbon dioxide is not a hazardous waste or pollutant; it's a natural component of the air, and we produce it simply by breathing. Moreover, our entire way of living is built around a carbon-based economy, which means most of what we do results in pumping out carbon dioxide. To address this issue, we must recognize that there is no way to resolve the current climate crisis while continuing our current lifestyle.

The simplest, most effective, and most sustainable way to address this problem is to reduce waste in our lives. Expecting companies to cut production and profits for the planet's sake is unrealistic. The real power to drive change lies with each of us as consumers. The most powerful and impactful action we can take is to practice reusing and recycling, eliminating unnecessary consumption, and allowing others to use what we don't need. These practices go beyond just reducing our carbon footprint; they make our lives simpler, our environment healthier, and our communities more caring, safer, and sustainable.

Cutting down our energy usage is also crucial to reducing our carbon footprint. While we have alternative energy sources like wind, tidal, and nuclear power, over 80 percent of our energy still relies on burning fossil fuels. For instance, driving a car emits about 400 grams of carbon dioxide per mile. In a 10-mile drive, that's 4 kilograms. Even the energy used for heating and cooling mostly comes from burning carbon, resulting in unavoidable carbon dioxide emissions.

Taking action to save energy daily can make a big difference. Simple steps like combining errands to reduce car usage, using light or motion sensors to avoid unnecessary lighting, and maintaining heating and cooling systems at optimal levels can go a long way.

Scientists are actively researching greenhouse gas reduction and the Earth's rising temperatures, leading to the development of new technologies. Innovations like capturing carbon from the atmosphere and storing it in the ground, or reducing sunlight by sprinkling highly reflective metal powder in the upper atmosphere, are being explored. However, it's ironic that while we discuss these solutions, we're still destroying natural greens, including precious tropical forests.

Maintaining and increasing natural forests is the safest, most natural, and most sustainable way to reduce atmospheric carbon dioxide. It's not just about rainforests like the Amazon; we can make this change anywhere in our living environment. Planting a few more trees in our yards or creating green spaces in apartment complexes can have a positive impact. This solution not only helps in reducing carbon dioxide but also contributes to a healthier living environment. Greenery has been an effective system for regulating atmospheric temperature for millions of years on our planet.

Saving water

Conserving water is crucial in addressing the current environmental crisis, alongside reducing carbon dioxide emissions. Seventy percent of the Earth's surface is covered by water, and the total amount of water on Earth remains constant. This fact made a global water shortage unimaginable half a century ago. However, of all the water on Earth, only about 3 percent is freshwater, with two-thirds locked in glaciers and inaccessible for direct use. In essence, only 1 percent of the water is available for the world's population.

Even this small percentage was not a significant issue when the Earth's water cycle was functioning normally. However, the rising temperatures in the atmosphere and seawater have seriously disrupted the water cycle. Consequently, we now experience more frequent and severe droughts and floods, significantly reducing water availability.

The changing climate also affects the groundwater supply, as water spends less time in the ground due to climate extremes. Consequently, many areas face a severe problem of groundwater depletion, as we increasingly rely on it for our water needs. Approximately 10 percent of the world's population doesn't have access to clean drinking water. An astounding 2.7 billion people are already facing water shortages. If current trends continue, by 2025, over two-thirds of the world's population could be dealing with water scarcity.

The water cycle disruption leading to a shortage of fresh water isn't just about people facing water scarcity; it has far-reaching consequences. It can result in the destruction of ecosystems, trigger wide-spread epidemics, and hamper food production. Just like we all breathe the same air, everyone is part of the Earth's great water cycle. So, whether it happens quickly or gradually, everyone will be impacted by the disturbance of the water cycle and the subsequent water shortage.

In the US, some states, including California, Nevada, and Arizona, are taking steps to conserve water. For new homes, they don't allow grass lawns. They also have policies prohibiting washing cars at home and limiting garden irrigation time.

Conserving water is as simple as putting a little thought into our daily habits. Easy actions like using a cup when brushing your teeth, turning off the water while soaping in the shower, or using a basin when washing your face can make a big difference. There are countless ways to reduce water usage without expensive technology or equipment, and they won't compromise our quality of life. These practices ensure water is used wisely and efficiently wherever it's needed. Best of all, they don't require special knowledge or skills, and anyone can do them with just a little attention.

Protecting biodiversity

Another vital aspect we can't ignore is protecting and promoting biodiversity. It's a big environmental issue that goes hand in hand with climate change. The decline in biodiversity is worsened by planting specifically selected varieties of crops and fruits to increase yields while other species are left out. For example, in the world market, only 1–2 species of bananas dominate. The same goes for soybeans and wheat. Using machinery and chemicals in farming for these limited varieties also leads to soil loss and degradation. If these crops don't have natural defenses against diseases and pests, it can cause a huge drop in production and even trigger a global food crisis.

An even more significant loss of biodiversity is occurring on a vast scale worldwide, often unnoticed, as a result of unintentional actions in forests, on land, and in rivers and oceans. From tiny microorganisms like bacteria and fungi in the soil to essential plankton in the oceans to majestic creatures like whales and tigers, numerous species are under serious threat due to human-driven changes in nature.

Currently, Earth is home to approximately 8 million species. As the environment changes, some species vanish while new ones emerge. We all know and cherish iconic endangered animals like tigers, whales, rhinoceroses, and pandas, which receive special protection. However, these beloved creatures represent just a tiny portion of the endangered species facing the destructive consequences of environmental changes. Beyond our attention, thousands of animals and plants are suffering and disappearing.

According to recent reports on biodiversity, approximately 15,000 species are currently considered endangered. Calculating the exact extinction rate is challenging due to the ever-changing nature of ecosystems and species. Scientists often refer to the fossil record to estimate the natural extinction rate, roughly 1 in 1 million species per year. Alarming data shows that the current extinction rate is more than 1,000 times higher than what occurs naturally.

Species diversity is crucial for strengthening the web of an ecosystem and making it more resilient to disturbances. When we examine the total biomass of mammals on Earth, it becomes clear that our current ecological net is dangerously fragile. When humans first appeared, we were just one of many mammals competing for resources and habitat. However, today, humans make up a striking 34 percent of the total biomass of mammals on Earth, exceeding all other species. And livestock raised by humans accounts for 62 percent of the total biomass. Humans and livestock make up 96 percent, leaving only 4 percent for wild mammals in their natural habitats.

The web of life woven by countless species and their interactions is incredibly vast and intricate, far beyond our comprehension. Within this complexity, we often don't fully understand how one species affects another. Our best approach is to preserve and not disrupt this delicate net for short-term gains. We should respect and safeguard this living system and seek ways to minimize our impact on it. This principle extends beyond protecting endangered species; it involves minimizing chemical usage, reducing household waste, promoting sustainable farming, increasing recycling, and embracing composting practices throughout our daily lives.

PRACTICE GUIDELINES
FOR HARMONY WITH NATURE

Save energy: Turn off lights and electronics when not in use, use energy-efficient appliances and LED light bulbs, and install programmable thermostats. Maintain indoor temperatures around 78°F in summer and 68°F in winter.

Conserve water: Fix leaks, use water-efficient fixtures, collect rainwater for outdoor use, and be mindful of water usage while washing dishes, taking showers, or watering plants.

Practice sustainable transportation: Opt for eco-friendly transportation such as walking, cycling, or public transit whenever possible. If owning a vehicle is necessary, consider electric or hybrid options.

Reduce single-use items: Minimize plastic bag, cup, and utensil use. Embrace reusable tumblers and shopping bags, and opt for used products. Avoid disposable spoons and forks for food delivery orders.

Conserve and recycle: Use items sparingly and handle them with care. Share or trade infrequently used items before they go to waste. Practice proper waste separation for recycling.

Reduce food waste: Practice meal planning, proper food storage, and repurposing leftovers. Donate excess food or compost scraps instead of throwing them away.

Support local and sustainable food: Choose local, organic, and seasonal foods to reduce the carbon footprint. Support local farmers' markets or plant a garden at home or in the community.

Protect natural habitats: Refrain from littering in natural areas and avoid actions that harm wildlife. Support conservation organizations and volunteer for habitat restoration projects.

Embrace regular Earth Hour practices: Dedicate time each month, week, or day to turn off lights, conserve water, reduce waste, make compost, plant trees, and support environmental movements.

Promoting Peace and Harmonious Coexistence

We promote peace and harmonious coexistence by fostering dialogue, respect, and understanding across cultures, religions, and nations.

The crisis we're facing right now can't be solved by one person, group, or country alone. We need international solidarity and cooperation to tackle it together. The environment knows no borders—rivers flow across nations, and natural disasters don't discriminate. Technology can help us work together better. What hinders cooperation is collective selfishness driven by short-term political and economic interests and old customs and notions that create barriers between us.

Differences among religious customs and notions may be the most difficult to resolve among all the challenges. The debate over religion is often fruitless and unproductive, with no clear resolution. Determining which religion is more truthful or which God is the true God through debate alone will unlikely lead to a definitive answer unless one side prevails by force. However, history has shown us that attempts to impose beliefs through force only breed more resentment and violence rather than providing a real solution to the problem.

The key to resolving differences is not to eliminate them but to acknowledge and embrace them. The current environmental crisis presents both risks and opportunities. It compels all countries, regardless of religious beliefs or cultural customs, to dialogue and find common ground. By talking and understanding each other's perspectives, we can build trust and work collaboratively to address the issues at hand. Through this process, we learn to live with and appreciate our differences, seeing them as valuable diversity rather than a cause of conflict.

The key to coexistence is shared common values. This fact is undoubtedly apparent to those who approach things rationally and with common sense. One such value that applies universally to all people, countries, and communities is the Earth itself. While the Earth has always been a shared value, people could not fully acknowledge its true significance in the past because there were no perceivable threats to this value, or we couldn't recognize the dangers even when we had them in front of our eyes. As a result, it didn't receive the attention and importance it rightfully deserved.

Now it's a different situation, and our Earth is seriously at risk. When this shared value, the Earth itself, is compromised, it undermines the foundation of all the other values we cherish—our personal success, our family's well-being, the growth of organizations and businesses, and the progress of nations and peoples.

To protect the value of our Earth, which forms the basis of all these precious values, we must come together and communicate, even with our differences. We have no choice but to cooperate and find common ground because the consequences of inaction are too grave.

The principle of coexistence is simple. It's about acknowledging and accepting that people with different opinions from me have the same value and right to exist in this world, no more and no less than I do. Even if everything is opposite, from how we eat to our political leanings, we share a common value— our Earth. This is the principle of coexistence and the common sense of a new humanity.

PRACTICE GUIDELINES FOR PEACE AND COEXISTENCE

Be kind: Embrace kindness by treating others with respect, compassion, openness, and empathy, regardless of any differences.

Practice self-kindness: Extend kindness to yourself. Prioritize your well-being with self-care, forgiveness, and self-compassion.

Embrace diversity: Celebrate and appreciate the diversity of cultures, religions, and perspectives around you. Challenge stereotypes or prejudices.

Practice active listening: Truly listen to others without interruption or judgment. Show genuine interest in their experiences, thoughts, and feelings.

Be mindful of the impact of your words and actions: Choose kindness in your communication, avoiding harmful or offensive language. Strive to uplift those around you.

Practice forgiveness: Let go of grudges toward others. Release resentment and foster understanding, and offer second chances.

Stand against bullying or discrimination: Speak up when you witness mistreatment and support those targeted. Foster a culture of respect and inclusion.

Volunteer and engage in service: Get involved in community projects, humanitarian initiatives, or cross-cultural programs. Build connections and bridge gaps.

Responsible Use of Technology and Sustainable Development

We support the mindful use of technology and sustainable and equitable economic development through responsible consumption, production, and investment.

In today's business world, sustainability is a must. Management principles focusing on eco-friendly products, reducing carbon footprint, and being environmentally responsible are now common knowledge for almost all businesses. Consumers are actively choosing products and services that align with these principles, making it challenging for businesses that don't follow sustainable practices to be selected.

The driving force behind this positive change isn't some visionary entrepreneur who had a sudden revelation. It's the power of consumers like us who make conscious choices for products, services, and companies that prioritize sustainability. That's what makes this change so encouraging and hopeful. It shows us how much influence our individual choices can have in shaping a better world. Moreover, these choices aren't made systematically like political decisions during elections. Instead, they come from very personal actions, such as taking a second look at labels and examining the country of origin, material, or manufacturing method with interest when choosing an item in the market.

Often, our choices are driven by personal gain rather than the greater cause of protecting the Earth. For instance, when choosing clothes made from natural materials or organic products, we may prioritize items that are less harmful to our bodies. However, regardless of the motive, the power of choice is at play.

Every time we select an item and scan its barcode at the checkout, we cast a vote. Companies closely observe these choices to understand consumer preferences. Depending on this information, they adjust production, discontinue certain products, and launch new ones.

Consumers' choices and evaluations hold immense power in determining the fate of a business in today's market. No business dares to be indifferent to consumer preferences because they know its influence. Even if these choices are made for personal benefit and not in an organized manner, they can still transform a company and significantly impact the market. Imagine if this power of choice is harnessed and organized around a common goal. There's nothing we can't change—whether it's a product, a business, an organization, or even a government.

Consumer choice holds tremendous power, reaching beyond everyday products like groceries or clothing. Yet, one area where we often underestimate our influence is in the realm of information. Whenever we click on a photo, video, news article, or social media post, we shape the content we encounter. Collectively, these individual choices steer the course of technology development and the content of information across the Internet.

While we may sometimes feel overwhelmed by the influence of big tech, the truth is that big tech relies on our attention. They try to capture and keep us engaged at all costs. It's not just the advanced technology of big tech that gives them power, but our own choices as users.

Online information is purposefully designed to do one thing—grab our attention. It's akin to using bait for hunting or fishing; at times, it's similar to feeding domestic animals. Platforms relentlessly bombard us with content to keep us engaged and consuming more information. By doing so, they boost the likelihood of us making a purchase or taking specific actions.

That's why being conscious of how we consume information, just like when we make mindful choices at the market, can have a significant impact. But a simple yet powerful action that can make an even more substantial difference is reducing the time spent on digital devices. Instead of being glued to screens, we can use the time to go for walks, cook, or connect with neighbors. A change like this benefits our health, strengthens community bonds, and even helps the planet by reducing energy use in data centers.

What if this trend of reducing digital device usage spreads like a fad on a large scale? For instance, what would happen if all users decided to stop using a specific platform for just one day? It would create a panic for the tech company. It's not just about that one day; it clearly demonstrates the immense potential of awakened and organized consumer choices.

We can apply the power of conscious choice in our consumption of goods and information and in more significant decisions like supporting political candidates and choosing where to work or live. The ability to make choices has always been there, but what truly matters is using this power consciously. The key is to make choices that benefit ourselves, others, and the planet, rather than seeking short-term and self-centered gains. By making these thoughtful choices, we can influence companies, communities, and countries to prioritize sustainability in their investments, developments, and policies.

Equality or fairness is a vital aspect that supports sustainability. The ones who bear the brunt of climate change and environmental degradation are often the least economically developed individuals or countries with low income and consumption. The people or nations with the largest carbon footprints do not suffer the most impact. Instead, those with the smallest carbon footprint, with the least influence on climate change, face the harshest consequences. They live in impoverished conditions, lacking the resources and systems to respond to climate change effectively. The current outcomes of climate change are inherently unfair, creating an unequal burden on vulnerable communities and regions.

According to the Global Carbon Project's 2021 statistics, the countries with the highest annual CO_2 emissions are China, the United States, India, and Russia, in that order. However, when considering yearly emissions per person, the United States leads with 14.86 tons, China with 8.05 tons (about half of the United States), and India with 1.93 tons (approximately one-eighth of the United States). The world average is 4.69 tons.

Regional comparisons also reveal significant differences in carbon emissions. High-income countries in North America, Europe, and East Asia, comprising 16 percent of the world's population, are responsible for 38 percent of carbon emissions. On the other hand, low-income countries in Africa, South America, and Southeast Asia, making up 50 percent of the global population, contribute only 14 percent of the total carbon emissions.

The most affected by this unfair outcome are individuals or groups who suffer the most and experience the damage firsthand. Unfortunately, their current living conditions often make it challenging to adopt sustainable practices, creating a barrier to achieving global sustainability. Fairness must be a fundamental consideration in plans and strategies for sustainable development and growth to achieve global sustainability. This responsibility cannot be left in the hands of economically disadvantaged individuals or countries. Instead, it calls for collective action from awakened, conscientious consumers and everyone willing to wield their power of choice to create a more just and sustainable world.

PRACTICE GUIDELINES FOR RESPONSIBLE USE OF TECHNOLOGY AND SUSTAINABLE DEVELOPMENT

Reduce screen time: Be aware of the potential harm of excessive digital device usage to mental health. Reduce digital device usage, and set specific breaks from screens during the day.

Prioritize offline activities: Prioritize screen-free activities daily such as exercise, hobbies, nature, books, and face-to-face connections. Balance technology for a healthier lifestyle.

Extend device life and recycle responsibly: Treat your devices carefully, opting for repairs over replacements. Avoid tossing them simply due to boredom or outdatedness; consider recycling through second-hand markets instead.

Invest responsibly: Invest responsibly by choosing sustainable and socially responsible investment options that align with your values.

Support circular economy initiatives: Choose brands that prioritize recycling, reuse, and repurposing through recycling programs, take-back programs, and product stewardship.

Support ethical brands: Support ethical and sustainable brands that prioritize fair trade, transparent supply chains, and environmental responsibility.

Educating Ourselves and Others

We educate ourselves and others about the urgent need for change, the opportunities for action, and stories of success and encourage others to join us in the effort to save the planet.

Unlike daily weather changes, the way climate change unfolds can be unnoticeable due to the limitations of our senses compared to the vast Earth climate system. For instance, in arid regions, we experience substantial daily temperature differences, sometimes 20–30 degrees, during seasonal shifts. As a result, people respond promptly by using air conditioning or adjusting clothing accordingly.

However, when it comes to gradual changes like 1 degree, 1.5 degrees, or 2 degrees over several decades or centuries, they become challenging to perceive directly. The Earth's system is immense, and alterations occur gradually, making them easy to overlook.

Unfortunately, once these changes begin, they are equally challenging to reverse. If we wait until the effects are easily noticeable, it may be too late, like a frog in a pot slowly boiling to death without realizing the temperature is rising.

In the late 1980s, climate warming and the thinning ozone layer started gaining attention and became public concerns. However, it took over 30 years for governments worldwide to fully grasp the urgency of the situation, as evident in the recent IPCC report. During these three decades, the focus has been on talking, debating, and persuading to build a shared understanding of climate change rather than implementing concrete solutions to address the problem.

The Paris Agreement aims to limit the temperature increase to 1.5 degrees, but achieving this target is challenging. Experts predict it could realistically rise to 2 degrees due to the Earth's complex climate system and its delayed response. To prevent this temperature increase, global action for change must happen now, simultaneously worldwide. If we spend the next 30 years as we did in the past, the Earth's atmosphere could warm by 2.5 degrees or more, leading to catastrophic consequences we cannot bear.

Making these changes may require revising our beliefs or value system, and it could even mean giving up certain comforts or profits we enjoy. This change is unlikely to begin spontaneously from entrepreneurs or politicians. It starts with conscious consumers and voters who are aware of the problem and committed to making a difference. As their voices demanding societal changes grow louder, businesses and politicians will feel compelled to take action.

Even with so much information available, many people are still unaware or indifferent about the severity of climate change. We might get concerned when we experience extreme weather events like hurricanes, heatwaves, floods, and droughts, but it tends to slip from our minds after a few days. The connection between these events and the urgent need for concrete actions to address climate change is often overlooked.

Everyone plays an indispensable role in responding to the global climate change crisis—including us. Those who recognize their responsibility as stewards of the planet and prioritize sustainability must lead the way. They understand that the Earth is the foundation of all values and proudly identify themselves as Earth Citizens. These individuals think and act with the Earth at the center of their value system, willingly putting aside personal interests when necessary for the greater good. They are the ones the Earth desperately needs; they are the new humanity.

In this critical moment, the new humanity requires many individuals with awareness and determination. If you resonate with this vision, actively engage with those around you, share your insights, and inspire their involvement. Countless avenues are available to achieve this goal. Consider starting by taking the New Humanity Pledge, which lies at the heart of this book's purpose.

Utilize your connections, platforms, workplaces, social groups, and media—all valuable stages and tools for your efforts. Your current location and environment are the perfect space for your actions. As you initiate conversations, exchange ideas, spread positivity, and connect with like-minded individuals, your efforts will gain momentum, influence, and power.

There are many ways to organize and maximize our impact in tackling environmental challenges. Established environmental organizations can lead the way, engaging the public in action-oriented efforts. Meanwhile, local community groups like schools, churches, and residents' associations can champion environmental initiatives in their areas. In addition to traditional organizations, we have the exciting potential of Decentralized Autonomous Organizations (DAOs) to drive solidarity and action without being constrained by time and space. These innovative platforms use decentralized, transparent decision-making, ensuring everyone's voice is valued. Combining DAOs with cutting-edge technologies like blockchain and the metaverse can create a new humanity community in the digital realm. This community can connect like-minded individuals from all over the globe, enabling collaboration to make a real difference in addressing global challenges.

PRACTICE GUIDELINES FOR EDUCATION AND SOLIDARITY

Be a role model: Set an example by living the new humanity's lifestyle in your daily life. Show through your actions how to prioritize self-care, foster meaningful relationships with others and nature, and make responsible choices in using technology and making investments.

Keep learning: Stay informed about environmental issues and sustainability by following reputable sources, reading books, watching videos, and attending lectures or webinars.

Start conversations: Engage others in conversations about natural health, environmental issues, and coexistence, sharing personal experiences, facts, and stories to inspire action.

Spread positive news: Share uplifting success stories and positive news that inspire hope and strength in creating a sustainable world.

Host film screenings or book clubs: Organize environmental film screenings or book clubs to spark discussions and inspire action on pressing issues and their solutions.

Support coexistence organizations: Offer your support to organizations working in environmental, peace, relief, and educational fields through volunteering or donations.

Promote the New Humanity Pledge: Share the pledge with your family, friends, and colleagues, encouraging them to join and embrace the guidelines of a new humanity.

* * * * *

The actions we've discussed are only the beginning; endless effective methods are waiting to be discovered, customized to fit each individual's life, passions, and strengths. The potential is limitless when we're committed to making a difference. With the vast array of technologies and resources available, we have the tools to amplify our impact. Even in the face of challenges, we view them as opportunities for growth and transformation, knowing that the current crisis catalyzes a more enlightened humanity and a thriving planet. At the core of this movement, you represent the new humanity of the 21st century—the architects of a better future.

CHAPTER 5

The New Humanity Pledge

The inception of the New Humanity Pledge defied logic; it was a sudden revelation that Earth needed a new humanity urgently. This feeling consumed me, and as I shared it with others and explored its meaning, the New Humanity Pledge emerged. While delving into logical explanations and adding daily practices for action, the original idea has become a book. Though this book seeks to offer rational explanations, its core lies in this one idea: a new humanity. It flooded my mind with powerful images, feelings, and urgency—a message from our distressed planet.

This book is not about conveying more information or logic; it's about igniting that same feeling of urgency, responsibility, and determination within you. What we need now, more than ever, are practical actions. It's the essence of this book, from start to finish.

If your heart dreams of a more peaceful and sustainable world and yearns to change the world and protect our Earth, then you are the embodiment of the new humanity. You hold the full text of the New Humanity Pledge, and as awakened individuals, let's walk this path together, inspiring more to join our cause and become part of the new humanity.

NEW HUMANITY PLEDGE

Why a New Humanity Must Rise

The unprecedented changes we are facing in our natural and social environments require a transformation of who we are and how we live. Therefore, we call for the birth of a new humanity. A new humankind that recognizes the interconnectedness of all life and makes the planet's well-being the foundation of all its values is urgently needed.

As *Homo sapiens*, our intelligence has helped us accomplish much, but it's not enough to solve the challenges we face as a planet. To overcome them, we must expand our consciousness and transform into *Homo coexistence*, a species that lives in harmony with the Earth, nature, and all life. If we don't choose coexistence, we will bring about our own destruction. The time to shift is now.

Change Is Urgent and Inevitable

Humanity stands at a crossroads. Worsening climate change, ecological collapse, uncontrollable technological advancements, and the increasing threat of violent conflict make it clear that time is running out for our species. We must take immediate action to turn things around. We need to undergo a radical shift in our thinking and behavior to address these challenges.

There Is a Better Story

While humanity has a history of competing and struggling for dominance, causing suffering to individuals and devastation to the planet, we must recognize that this is not our only story. Our true story, one of greatness and beauty, has yet to be written. The choice and power to shape our destiny is in our own hands, now more than ever.

We Are Ready

The answers to our problems are already available to us. What we need is to make a choice and commitment. If we are concerned about the future of humanity and our planet, if we're dedicated to leaving the Earth in a better state than it is now, if each of us is willing to play our role in contributing to a future that is sustainable, just, and peaceful, then we are ready to transform ourselves into a new kind of humanity.

We Choose Who We Are

We recognize that we are not bound by any dogma, religion, or limiting belief system. By breaking free from the constraints of the past, we take ownership of our bodies, minds, and consciousness, and we create a new path toward a more peaceful and sustainable future.

We Are Earth Citizens

We recognize that we are citizens of the world, transcending skin color, language, race, culture, religion, and nationality. We understand that we share a common identity as inhabitants of this planet. We are committed to fostering the health of the Earth and all life and to promoting harmonious coexistence with each other and the Earth.

We Are Nature

We recognize that we are not separate from nature but an integral part of it. We understand that our actions have a profound impact on the natural world. By embracing our natural essence, we restore our connection with nature and work toward creating a healthier relationship with our planet.

We Are the Earth's Future

We recognize that the Earth's future is not someone else's problem but the responsibility of each of us to protect and preserve. By embracing this responsibility, we can create a sustainable and thriving future for our planet and all its residents.

Proposed Actions

As members of a new humanity, we commit ourselves to the following actions:

1. Caring for our own physical, mental, and emotional wellness naturally and proactively whenever possible and helping others do the same.

2. Living in harmony with nature by reducing our carbon footprint, conserving energy and water, and protecting natural habitats and biodiversity.

3. Promoting peace and harmonious coexistence by fostering dialogue, respect, and understanding across cultures, religions, and nations.

4. Supporting mindful use of technology and sustainable and equitable economic development through responsible consumption, production, and investment.

5. Educating ourselves and others about the urgent need for change, the opportunities for action, and stories of success, and encouraging others to join us in the effort to save the planet.

A Call for a New Humanity

We urge everyone, from individuals to organizations and governments, to prioritize the well-being of our planet and all its inhabitants above short-term profit, convenience, and power. Let us unite and take the first step toward changing our past habits and ideas and building a new humanity committed to harmonious coexistence with each other and our planet.

"I pledge to become part of a new humanity and to make creating coexistence on Earth my personal responsibility and priority."

Visit www.NewHumanityPledge.org
to take the pledge.

Acknowledgments

I extend my heartfelt gratitude to Steve Kim, my dedicated partner, whose collaborative spirit breathed new life into the concepts of this book. I am also indebted to Nicole Dean for refining the manuscript and enhancing its readability. Kiryl Lysenka's design expertise has elevated the book.

I am grateful to the remarkable team at my US publisher, Best Life Media, whose unwavering support and dedication have been instrumental in bringing this book to fruition.

Lastly, I want to thank all the Earth Citizens around the world for their hard work in creating a more peaceful, mindful, and sustainable world. Your efforts have truly shaped the essence of this work.

Resources

New Humanity Pledge Website

This website hosts the New Humanity Pledge, where individuals can formally take the pledge. The pledge focuses on prioritizing our planet and its people, fostering harmony, and sustainable living through personal responsibility and collective action. To learn more, visit NewHumanityPledge.org.

Ilchi Lee's Email Newsletter

Ilchi Lee sends weekly inspirational messages, tips, and meditations on how to live a life of coexistence and fulfillment. Get ongoing advice and encouragement for connecting with your heart and mind and using them to create a bright future. Sign up at Ilchi.com/newsletter.

Earth Citizens Organization (ECO)

This nonprofit founded by Ilchi Lee promotes mindful living and natural health for a sustainable world. It provides leadership programs that develop individuals' skills and strengths to foster an Earth Citizen lifestyle in communities. It also runs the ECO Farm, which offers programs that deliver practical skills that connect food and wellness. To learn more, visit EarthCitizens.org.

Body & Brain Yoga and Tai Chi Classes

Find classes with expert instructors in yoga, tai chi, and meditation at Body & Brain Yoga Tai Chi centers. There are about 80 centers across the United States, with more in South Korea, Japan, Europe, Canada, and New Zealand. Group classes, workshops, and individual sessions are available both online and offline. Find a US center near you at BodynBrain.com.

Books of Related Interest

The Art of Coexistence:
How You and I Can Save
the World

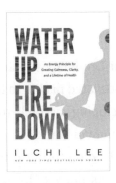

Water Up Fire Down:
An Energy Principle for
Creating Calmness, Clarity,
and a Lifetime of Health

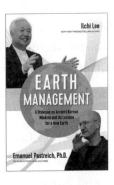

Earth Management:
A Dialogue on Ancient
Korean Wisdom and Its
Lessons for a New Earth

Change: Realizing Your
Greatest Potential

About the Author

Ilchi Lee is a visionary, mentor, and educator who has devoted his life to teaching energy principles and developing methods to nurture the full potential of the human brain.

He developed mind-body training methods such as Body & Brain Yoga and Brain Education, which have inspired many people worldwide to live healthier and happier lives. He also founded the undergraduate Global Cyber University and the graduate University of Brain Education.

Lee has penned more than 40 books, including the *New York Times* bestseller *The Call of Sedona: Journey of the Heart*, as well as *The Art of Coexistence: How You and I Can Save the World*.

A well-respected humanitarian, Ilchi Lee has founded nonprofits such as the International Brain Education Association (IBREA) and Earth Citizens Organization (ECO). For more information about Ilchi Lee, visit Ilchi.com.